J Is For Jump!

Moving into Language Skills

Maya Doray

A Fearon Teacher-Aid Book

Fearon Teacher Aids
a division of
PITMAN LEARNING, INC.
Belmont, California

I would like to dedicate this book to children and to teachers of children everywhere to bring them added joy through movement and through the perception of beauty that is all around them.

I would also like to express my gratitude to Bernadette Hecox, M.A., R.P.T., assistant professor in Program in Physical Therapy at Columbia University in New York, for her enthusiasm and help as well as her continuous encouragement in my work.

Editorial director: Roberta Suid
Editor: Kate Fuller
Production manager: Suzanne Olver
Text and cover designer: Susan True
Illustrator: Maya Doray
Photographer: Irene Stern
Manufacturing manager: Susan Fox

ISBN−0−8224−4004−0
Library of Congress Catalog Card Number: 81−85350
Printed in the United States of America.
1.9 8 7 6 5 4 3

PREFACE

Dear Teacher,

After many years of dancing and choreographing, I had the opportunity to present several of my children's productions to dance teachers at a national convention. The response was enthusiastic, largely due to my use of creative movement rather than formal or conventional methods. This response made me realize the value for teachers of children moving creatively. Children also benefit from this activity—they enjoy it, and it can enrich their educational experience and allow them to express themselves fully. Since that time, I have turned my attention to teachers and children. Nowhere can creative movement be used as productively as in the classroom.

This book was written with you, the teacher, in mind. Its purpose is to help you use movement in your classroom so that children can have fun as they explore and learn various fundamentals of reading and writing. The terms and concepts treated in this book are derived from standard academic approaches. I have converted into movement terms as many aspects of language fundamentals as possible; you can incorporate these into your curriculum material for use in your classroom.

The format of this book enables you to lead professional movement classes from the start, whether or not you have ever taken or taught a movement class before. The wording used in the text is that which has proven most effective for drawing an instant response from the many children with whom I have worked. It will give you confidence in teaching the material, and help you avoid the pitfalls that can result from a wrong or a poor presentation. The guidelines in the introduction give you practical suggestions for getting started using creative movement in your classroom.

I hope this book will bring you and your students many hours of enjoyment, and I am confident that the results will be your ultimate and greatest reward.

Maya Doray
New York, NY

CONTENTS

GUIDELINES FOR TEACHERS

Many people think of movement only in terms of recreation or physical achievement. However, especially for young children, movement is the very essence of life, and joy in moving is inherent in all children everywhere. Because it is such a powerful factor in their lives, movement—when geared toward a specific subject—has great potential as a teaching tool for youngsters. Applied in this way, creative movement lets children learn in a way that incorporates their natural propensity for physical activity.

WHAT IS CREATIVE MOVEMENT?

To a great many people not familiar with dance and movement education, the term *creative movement* seems to imply jumping around freely and aimlessly. However, this is not so—freedom alone does not induce creativity, nor has anything of worth ever been achieved through a sudden, unguided burst of energy alone. Just as an art teacher must introduce various tools to children, illustrate their use, and then provide a project on which the children can work in order to create something of their own, so must the movement teacher guide children toward definite goals and help them manage their tools. In this case, the tools are the basics of movement education and dance—Steps and Body Moves, plus the elements Time, Space, and Force.

   The body can move in a great many ways. A specific movement, modified by the addition of time, space, or force elements, gives us the structure for creative movement. For example, a child might walk with: an added time element, such as quick or slow steps; an added space element, such as a specific direction, pathway, or design; or a specific force element, such as heavy or dainty steps. The walk can be further modified by using such elements in different combinations. Similarly, leg, arm, or body movements can be modified. Proper guidance allows the children to move freely while learning and having fun.

HOW CAN MOVEMENT BE RELATED TO LANGUAGE ARTS?

The basic elements of movement are related to fundamentals of language arts in several ways. Each letter of the alphabet is made of certain shapes that form a specific design; each letter also has a particular sound. These letters combine to form words, and the sounds and meanings of these words either specify or suggest images that can be interpreted through creative movement. Moving—as an expression of letters and words, sounds and meanings—provides a physical association that is extremely relevant to a child. This association helps children learn faster and also retain information more easily than they could otherwise. Enabling children to make this connection is the overall objective of this book, but within the various lessons are many different objectives. These are listed at the head of each lesson, and in the index for your easy reference.

ABOUT THE TEACHING METHOD

Movement can be taught in either of two ways: formally or creatively. In the formal approach, the children follow instructions at all times and carry them out uniformly. In the creative approach, which is used predominantly in this book, the children make choices to find their own solutions and to devise means of expressing them. The teacher's function is to lead and guide the children by giving examples, asking leading questions, setting up problems and challenges, and supplying certain limitations and reference points. Also required is a certain amount of formal instruction, which enables the children to do creative work by providing them with concrete technical "equipment."

All these requirements are met in the step-by-step, ready-to-teach format of the lessons. You are presented with not only the sequence but also the actual wording of instructions to the children. You can use these instructions verbatim or as an outline during each session. Every lesson contains all the necessary components of a well-rounded movement session, complete with diagrams and sketches to augment written explanations. Because the children must start out with some ideas and actual examples, nearly every activity includes a list of variations from which you can choose. Discussions, when appropriate, are developed that let you help the children come up with, and then implement, their own ideas.

The lessons within each section are graded: the easiest lesson comes first, and the subsequent lessons gradually increase in complexity. Use the lessons in each section consecutively; however, you may want to repeat some of the lesson material once you have completed a section. Each lesson contains a number of separate activities that form a balanced, unified movement session. These activities can easily be interchanged; just alternate "stationary" activities with "locomotor" activities to maintain the proper balance of the children's energy output. In this way you will be able to structure later lessons for variety, interchanging the materials to meet the needs of your own particular classroom.

The atmosphere, as the sample dialogues suggest, should be informal. However, to avoid lack of discipline and unnecessary noise, establish an explicit understanding with the children from the outset: It is their *bodies* that talk during these movement sessions, so their mouths should not talk at the same time. Also tell them that they will need to listen to you carefully because you will be giving them directions as they move. At the same time, encourage the children to have fun and enjoy themselves. If at all possible, participate with them. Your own enthusiasm and interest will be the children's best stimulus.

HOW MUCH SPACE WILL YOU NEED?

The material in this book is meant for classroom use. Clearing away some of the furniture should free up a space that is large enough for the class to participate all together—or, if necessary, in small groups. However, you may find a larger area elsewhere in the school, which you could use for 30 minutes once a week or so.

However, much of the material of this book is designed for a fairly constricted area, with the children sitting or standing in a circle. Therefore, if you do not have enough room for a given activity, you can skip it or exchange it with one from another lesson that is similar in type but that requires less space. Most studies can be adapted to fit a variety of situations.

Area permitting, all activities can be done as unified class activities (except where otherwise indicated). Most activities will work equally well if you divide the class into two groups; one group observes while the other participates, and then they change over. In such cases you may find it most comfortable to work with groups of 10 to 12 children.

GETTING STARTED

Every classroom situation is different, and every teacher needs to make certain adaptations. However, a few general guidelines may be helpful.

1. Read through the entire lesson to see what kind of activities it contains and what equipment, if any, you will need. If you have never done movement activities with your class, you might start out with only one or two of the activities from the first lesson. You can repeat these activities as part of the whole lesson, once you feel confident about holding longer sessions. Repetition is something children always enjoy—it lets them improve on their actions and thus gives them confidence.

2. Decide on the area you'll use, and set it up beforehand, if possible. If you will be using a record player, place it near you, against a wall, with the records nearby.

3. If the area you are using serves for a variety of activities, you may want to establish a standard way of starting creative movement sessions. This will help invoke the rules for these sessions without your having to repeat them every time. You might, for example, use a certain piece of music as a "signature" tune, or you might have the children assemble for the lesson in a specific way, perhaps as one special kind of animal. Rabbits are good because they are active and agile, but also very quiet. You might say, "All bunnies hop over here." Depending on the circumstances, you may prefer to use a drum or other percussion instrument to call the children together. You may want to let children take turns adding a few beats until everyone has arrived.

REGARDING FORMATION

The most suitable formation for young children is a circle of which you are a part, with occasional line-ups for going across the room. Sometimes the children are asked to spread out and stand facing you. Let them do so on their own; they will find their own spots readily enough. When the children need to form small groups of 4 to 6 children, let them take partners and then combine two or three pairs. To form larger groups, you can divide the class arbitrarily, or you can let the children sit in a circle and count off from 1 to 3 to make 3 groups, from 1 to 4 to make 4 groups, and so on. Then have all the ones work together inside the circle as the rest of the class watches, then all the twos, and so on. You will find explicit directions within the text for similar situations.

USING ACCOMPANIMENT

Your main and most important instrument is your voice. Use it not only to give directions, but also to add color, feeling, and dramatic impact. Clapping your hands can add special accents. Sometimes, however, and particularly for larger classes, an additional accompaniment is very helpful. This can be supplied either by a percussion instrument or by recorded music.

Which percussion instrument to select depends on your personal preference. Most teachers use a drum; my own preference is for a small tambourine, which can be used like a drum but is easier to handle. Whichever instrument you choose, practice using it beforehand.

Do *not* attempt using your instrument to accompany a locomotor activity (such as walking, running, skipping, and so on). Providing just the right accompaniment requires a great deal of practice and experience. You will mainly need an instrument to provide specific signals: to stop, to change formation, to occasionally take off for a leap, and to call the children together. You also will find suggestions to accompany short rhythmic movements with a percussive beat.

Music is a natural incentive to movement, and moving to music is a most satisfying experience. However, the music used as accompaniment must be carefully selected for rhythm and mood in order to supply the appropriate background. Two main categories of music are called for in this book: music for simple, usually quite short activities involving one basic step (skipping, hopping, and so on), and music for longer interpretations. Lively polkas, children's songs, marches, and folk dances are best suited for the former. Lyrical and romantic music of classical composers, Strauss waltzes, and ballet excerpts are best suited for the latter. General suggestions for types of music are listed in the various activities, where they are needed. More specific recommendations can be found in the Appendix.

Do not be afraid to let the children try an activity that seems "far out" to you, or hard to visualize. Children are wonderfully inventive and can readily express their imaginations through movement. All they need is a gentle push to get started, and that is what this book provides. So proceed with confidence. You will be providing the children with joyous, healthy activities that, at the same time, will lead you closer to your own teaching goals.

1
MOVING IS FUN!

This section is a springboard for the rest of the book. It introduces children to the basic concepts of time, space, and force as they relate to reading and writing. The lesson sequence leads them systematically through explorations and experiences with movement. The material also allows the teacher to become familiar with presenting movement sessions in general, and with using creative movement in particular. For best results, use the following lessons in consecutive order. After you have completed this section with your class, you may want to return to various parts of any of the lessons. They can be used over and over again in unrelated sessions.

1 Wriggling and Other Moves
(20–25 minutes)

Objective: To provide general movement experiences

Special Equipment: Record of music for skipping (optional)

SKIP! STOP! SKIP!   (2–2½ minutes) *locomotor*

Let the children skip freely around the room to music, if possible. At uneven intervals have them stop for a few seconds at your prearranged signal. The simplest signal is stopping the music, and then starting it again to signify "go." Otherwise use a clear percussive signal such as 2 or 3 drumbeats or a few hand claps. Whichever signal you choose, demonstrate it for the children before they start to skip.

Say:

When the music starts (*or* on my signal to go) **skip around the room** in your own way. Keep listening to the music (*or* for my signal to stop). **When the music stops** (*or* when you hear this signal) **you stop too.** Are you ready? Skip! (signal to stop) And skip! (and so on)

[handwritten note in right margin:] very young children ie age 3-4 cannot skip. they have not developed the motor coordination needed... they may hop

WHAT CAN YOU WRIGGLE? (6–7 minutes) *stationary*

Let the children try wriggling various parts of their bodies, first while standing, then while sitting in a circle. Start out by giving them simple ideas; then ask them for suggestions, taking those that are practicable and working on them one at a time. When necessary, add directions to these suggestions in order to expand small movements to incorporate the entire body.

Say:

> Make a large circle and **stand comfortably.** Now look at your hands. **Can you wriggle your fingers?** Can you wriggle them high above your head? Wriggle your fingers as you reach between your legs, way behind you. Now wriggle anywhere, all around yourself, in many different directions. **What else can you wriggle?**

Take children's suggestions one at a time. Ideas might be **an arm, a shoulder, both arms, both shoulders, the hips and tummy, the neck, or the toes.** After a while have the children sit down. Again, ask them for suggestions. This will give them a different movement experience.

Say:

> Now sit down and wriggle your **toes.** Can you wriggle them above your head? Can you wriggle your **hips** while you are sitting? Now lie down and wriggle your **whole self.** How else can you lie to do that? (on the stomach, on the side, or in a shoulder stand) What else can you wriggle?

HOW ELSE CAN YOU MOVE? (5–6 minutes) *stationary*

Call out various body parts, letting the children experiment to find different ways to move them. At the same time, suggest ideas and make comments to spur the children on.

Say:

> Sit up and let's find more things to do with different parts of our bodies. What can you do with your **hands?** (waving hello, punching, circling, and so on) What can you do with your **head?** With your **elbows?** With both **arms?** With your **whole body?** (bending, twisting, circling the trunk rolling back and forth, and so on) With both **legs?** Lie back and try out many different things.

Let the children work on their own for a while; then have them try out one another's ideas, such as kicking, bicycling, reaching to the ceiling, and so on. Have the children try moving their legs while standing before you go on to the next activity.

HOPPING ACROSS (3–4 minutes) *locomotor*

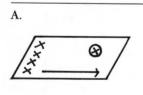
Have the children line up on one side of the room, cross over one at a time, then wait on the other side for your next instruction. Stand at the side about halfway down the room and face the children. The children can either go straight across or they can cross on the diagonal, as shown in figures A and B. In a very large area, stand in the center and have the children stop when they reach you (see figure C). Then they can walk to the other end of the room, or they can simply sit down near you to await their next turn. Start the children out one at a time by giving each one a signal such as "And!" or "Next!" or "Ready? Go!"

Say:

Line up, everyone, on this side of the room. (indicate) One at a time, **hop across with both feet together,** like a bird. I want each one of you to wait for my signal to start, and then to wait at the other side. Are you ready? Hop!

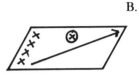

B.

Next have the children hop across on one leg and hop back on the other leg.

Say:

This time try hopping on just one leg at a time. If you want to, you can hold on to one ankle while you **hop across on one leg.** Go across one at a time. When you reach the other side, stop and wait. Are you ready? Hop!

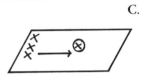

C.

BLANKET   (5–6 minutes) *stationary*

Have the children spread out across the room and find places to lie down. Ask them to pretend they are blankets covering someone up. The movements of the person underneath them make them wriggle in different places. Let your voice guide them as they move. Pause long enough between the sentences to allow the children to experiment with lifting themselves as they lie on the floor (see figure 1).

Say:

Spread out and find a place to lie down. **Make believe you are a blanket lying flat on the bed.** Suddenly you feel someone lifting up one of your corners, and you feel it being lifted higher and higher. Now someone is crawling right under you. You can feel the person wriggling around underneath you, moving about, lifting you here and there, and finally settling down right under your center. Suddenly you are being kicked off the bed and you fall to the floor all crumpled up! For a while you lie there in a heap; then someone picks you up, lifts you up high and shakes you out! Now the person puts you back, stretching you out flat and comfortably on your bed.

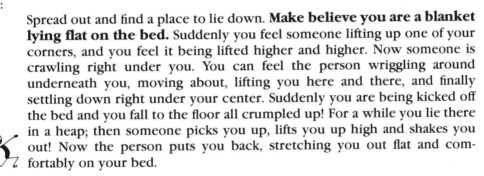

1.

You may want to repeat this activity, having the children lie on their stomachs instead of on their backs. If the class is small enough, you might walk around and touch the children at various points to make them lift themselves up here and there. Older children might try this with a partner later on.

CLOWN   (1–2 minutes) *locomotor*

For a quick change of pace, let the children get up and be clowns, jumping or moving in their own ways.

Say:

Everybody up on your feet. **Make believe you are a clown.** You can wriggle or jump or move in any way you like.

2 Saying Hello
(20–25 minutes)

Objectives: To provide experience working with partners; to provide general movement experiences

Special Equipment: Record of music for skipping

SKIP! STOP! MEET A PARTNER! (2–2½ minutes) *locomotor*

Have the children choose partners; then play the music and stop it at odd intervals. While the music is playing, the partners should separate and skip away from each other. When the music stops, the children should look for their partners and run to meet them. Make sure the children really disperse while they skip.

Say:

> **Everybody choose a partner. When the music starts** I want you to leave your partner and **skip all over the room alone. When the music stops,** you stop too for a moment to **look for your partner.** When you see each other, run together to **meet.** Are you ready? On your own, skip! (play the music) Stop! Meet your partners! And on your own again, skip! (and so on)

SAYING HELLO (5–7 minutes) *stationary*

Ask the children to sit down in a circle. Say hello to them with different parts of your body, calling out each part and making any move you like with it. Precede each move by saying, "I say hello to you with. . . ." The children are to answer you back by moving the same body part any way they wish.

Say:

> **Make a circle and sit down.** I am going to say hello to you, but not with my voice. I am going to use different parts of my body. You can answer me back using the same part I used, but you can use it in your own way. For example, **I might say hello to you with my head,** nodding it to you. Then **you answer me with your head,** doing whatever you like with it—shaking it, rolling it, and so on. Are you ready? Listen: I say hello to you with . . . my big toe. Now let me see **your** big toe say hi back to me. Now I say hello to you with my head. With my face. (blow or puff your cheeks or make a funny face) With my elbows. With my tummy. (and so on)

End by getting up and using your whole self, running in place or wriggling or shaking yourself.

FOLLOW THE LEADER (6–7 minutes) *stationary*

Continue the previous activity, this time letting children take turns being the leader. The rest of the class should copy the leader's movements rather than moving differently.

Say:

> You had so many good ideas, I think we should all have a look at them. **Sit down again and take turns showing one movement to the whole class.** This time we will all follow the leader. **Everyone will copy your movement** as you say hello and call out your body part. Who would like to start?

MEETING A FRIEND (8–10 minutes) *locomotor*

First let the children make believe they are bunnies while you suggest various movement ideas to them. Then let them work in pairs and make up little scenes of meeting one another (see figure 2).

Say:

 Make believe you are a bunny hopping around. Sometimes you run with tiny little steps. Then sometimes you stop to stroke your long soft ears, or to dig out and nibble a root of a plant. (demonstrate, if desired)

Suggest that the children hop and run in a fairly erect posture—crouching down is too strenuous and it limits movement. After a while, suggest that they work with partners.

Say:

 Take a partner and be two little bunnies together, meeting and greeting each other in a special way. You might tap your hands together, or hop around each other, shake your head and ears, or rub your noses together. Think up your own special way to say hello to your bunny friend. When you are ready we can all watch each couple.

When the children are ready, have them sit in two lines, facing their partners across the room. Then let one couple at a time meet in the center and perform their scene. Continue by letting them be other animals. Each time, suggest several ideas before the children begin to improvise.

Say:

 Now let's **think of two other animals meeting.** What do you think two birds would do when they meet?

Some ideas for animal actions:

- *Birds:* Hopping on one or both legs, flapping the wings, nodding their heads, chasing each other, and so on.
- *Kittens:* Cuddling close, playing together, rounding their backs, rolling over, jumping softly, and so on.
- *Puppies:* Lifting their paws, wagging their tails, wriggling their bodies, walking around each other, bouncing, and so on (erect, not crouching).
- *Bears:* Walking with heavy steps, perhaps on all fours, swaying from side to side, rearing up, sitting back to back, rolling over each other, and so on.

End this session by having the children again work in pairs to make up little scenes of animals meeting. Let the children choose the animals they wish to be; they can both be the same kind of animal or they each can choose to be a different kind of animal.

3 Forward and Backward
(20–25 minutes)

Objectives: To explore the directions *forward* and *backward;* to provide general movement experience.

WALKING FORWARD   (4–6 minutes) *locomotor*

Have the children cross the room several times in a group, each time doing a different step. Call out the step and give a go signal; have them wait at the other side for your next call.

3.

Say:

Everyone come to this side of the room. (indicate) On my signal, **walk over to the other side;** then wait for my next call. Are you ready? Walk!

Continue in this way, using any or all of the following suggestions: walking very **fast**; walking **on tiptoes** slowly and carefully; walking **on heels**; **running**; **marching** with knees raised high; marching with stiff legs; walking on all fours; **hopping** on one leg then on the other; **galloping** across the room and back again.

REACHING FORWARD AND BACKWARD   (5–7 minutes) *stationary*

Have the children stand in a circle. Ask them first to reach forward with various body parts, then to reach backward with various body parts. Encourage them to stretch as far as possible each time in order to get the maximum amount of movement from each action (see figure 3).

Say:

Stand in a large circle without holding hands. How far can you **reach forward with your arm?** Now try the **other arm**, reaching even further. See how far forward you can reach with your **head**. Now try reaching forward with your **knee**. Now with your **big toe**.

Reaching with the leg can be done in different ways. Let the children experiment; then point out various children's ideas for all to try. After a while go on to reaching backward (see figure 4).

Say:

Now let's try reaching backward. How could you **reach back with your arms?**

Reaching backward can be done in many ways. Let the children experiment.

Say:

Which way can you stretch further—with just one arm or with both arms together?

End by having the children sit down and reach backward and forward with their legs. Finally have them rock back and forth (see figure 5).

FORWARD AND BACKWARD STEPS   (5–7 minutes) *locomotor*

Have the children get up, spread out in the room, and stand facing you. Then call out various steps in fast succession, alternating between forward and backward directions. Give a stop signal at the end of each action in order to alert the children to your next call.

Say:

Spread out all over the room and **stand facing me.** I am going to call out **different steps** for you to do, either **forward or backward**, so listen very carefully. Are you ready?

Use any or all of the following suggestions: 1 jump forward; 3 jumps back, 2 giant steps forward; tiptoe back with tiny steps; kick one leg forward 3 times, now the other; kick one leg back 3 times, now the other; crawl forward, then back; stand up and look back through your legs; sit down and walk forward while sitting; get up and walk your hands forward and back without moving your feet; hop forward on one leg; jump forward with both feet together; hop forward with the other leg; march forward, then backward; jump back with both feet together; make a giant step back; walk 3 steps forward, then make 1 jump back.

End this activity by having the children all go to one side of the room and then cross over to the other side by continuously repeating this sequence of movements: *3 steps forward and 1 jump back*. If you wish, this activity can be repeated at another time as a race, with small groups of children competing. The children can count their own steps.

CASTING A SPELL   (5–6 minutes) *locomotor*

Tell the children you are going to pretend to have magic powers and to cast a spell over the room that will change it into a very different kind of place. Then have all the children go to one side of the room and cross to the other side in a group. Give them a different spell for each crossing. After you call out your spell the children can begin to cross, improvising their movements as they go. Elaborate on your spell as they are crossing in order to give them further ideas for movements they can do.

Say:

> Everyone stay on this side of the room. I am going to cast a magic spell that will change this entire room, and then you will have to reach the other side. When everyone is safely there, I am going to cast a new spell for you. Are you ready? I am changing this room into . . . a **meadow**! Make believe the sun is shining and there are lovely flowers to **smell and pick**, and butterflies you can **chase**, and soft green grass you can **jump and romp** about on your way to the other side.

Use any or all of the following spells:

- *Deep water:* So deep in some places that you can barely hold your head above it. You have to wade or paddle all the way across.
- *Hot sand:* Run quickly to the other side so you don't burn your feet. Then, when you are there, you can jump into the water to cool off.
- *Deep snow:* It is so deep that you have to pick your feet up high at every step you take. You can throw snowballs or build a snowman on your way across.
- *Dense fog:* So dense you can barely see, but you have to find your way to the other side. Step carefully, search, and guard your face—there are trees, and you feel the low branches brushing against you. Wander around until you are safely out on the other side.
- *A stage:* You are in a ballet—dancing, and turning, and jumping all the way across.
- *Slippery ice:* You can skate, and slide, and turn some more, and sometimes you slip and fall, but you finally make it to the other side.
- *A bouncy mattress:* And you jump and bounce and bounce, all the way home.

4 Making Shapes
(20–25 minutes)

Objectives: To develop spatial awareness and body image

Special Equipment: An 18-inch length of flexible wire (optional)

WALK! STOP! BE! (2½–3 minutes) *locomotor*

Have the children walk about freely, stopping at your signal and making the shape you call out for them. Make your stop signal loud and clear to alert the children to your next instruction. Do not let the children hold a position for too long or they may be uncomfortable.

Say:

Walk all around the room and on my signal (indicate) stop and listen, because **I will call out a shape for you to make**. Then **freeze for a moment** so that I can have a look at you. Ready? Walk. Stop. (signal) And be **small**. And walk. Stop. (signal) And be **fat**. And walk. (and so on)

Continue, using any or all of the following shapes: skinny; upside-down; crooked; leaning sideways; wide; narrow; twisted; tall; high and wide (and other combinations); funny; and so on. Repeat a few of these several times. End by letting the children make any shape they choose.

CHANGING SHAPES (5–7 minutes) *stationary*

6.

Continue to explore shapes. Start with everyone standing, and let the children change slowly from one shape to another (see figure 6).

Say:

Let's try some more shapes. Spread out and stand facing me. Now make yourself as **tiny** as you can. Very **slowly grow wider** and wider. Now be **tiny** again in another way. How else can you be tiny? **Slowly grow into a different wide shape**. You can rise if you like, to kneel or stand as you grow wide.

Let the children watch one another, perhaps by one half watching while the other half moves.

Use any or all of the following shapes: **a twisted shape** (repeat a few times), growing from small and low into high and twisted, spiking out in different places like a prickly thornbush; **upside-down and twisted**, lying with the feet in the air, or standing and bending over; **flat and slowly growing** into a prickly shape; **walking while in a twisted shape**; walking in other shapes, such as **stiff, fat, soft,** and **limp; sinking slowly** into a flat low shape and **quickly changing** to a round shape (repeat the fast change a few times).

RUN! STOP! DROP DOWN (1½–2 minutes) *locomotor*

For a fast change of pace, let the children get up, run about freely, and then drop down to the floor at your signal. Make a signal in addition to your voice call; it should be loud and clear. Repeat the sequence 5 or 6 times.

Say:

Everyone on your feet! **Run around the room,** anywhere you like, and when I give you this signal (demonstrate) **drop down** to the floor. Ready? Run! Drop down! And run! (and so on)

BE A WIRE (6–7 minutes) *stationary*

Ask the children to make believe they are pieces of wire that are being bent into different shapes. Try to get an actual piece of wire (such as picture-hanging wire).

Start out by showing the wire to the children, bending it in various ways, and perhaps passing it around so that the children can bend it themselves.

Say:

> **Make believe you are a piece of wire.** (show the wire) You are lying **all curled up** on the floor. Now someone comes and **slowly straightens you** out, a bit here, then a bit there, and yet in another place. Now you are straight. Then the person bends you again to give you **a new shape**, changing you again and again. Finally the person **twists you all up** and **drops you on the floor**.

Repeat this a few times, letting the children establish their own timing and movements in accordance with their own ideas. In smaller classes, you might let each child move while the others watch, until all the children are crumpled up in a heap at the end.

WEIRD CREATURES   (5–6 minutes) *locomotor*

Let the children make believe they are weird, strangely shaped creatures, each moving about in its own way.

Say:

> Let's do some more make believe. **Make believe you are a weird creature on a strange planet.** Each one has a different form and a different shape, and each moves in its own strange way. Some of you might be fat and blown up, and walk with a waddle while puffing along. Other creatures might hop and then turn around, making strange sounds; or someone might be long and thin with many spidery legs. Be any creature you like and move in your own way.

After they have experimented for a while, have the children watch each other, taking turns, either one or a few at a time.

---

5 Over and Under
(25–30 minutes)

Objectives: To explore the concepts over and under; to develop body image
Special Equipment: 1 sheet of construction paper for each child

RUN AND FREEZE   (2–2½ minutes) *locomotor*

Have the children run freely around the room, stopping at your signals and freezing in any shape they wish. Since the children have done this before, you don't need to make any initial comments. Have the children hold each position only for a few seconds; here, however, *do* make comments while they move—remind them to change from a high to a low position, and perhaps suggest a few interesting ideas. Have them make 6 to 7 changes.

Say:

> When I say go, **run around** the room anywhere you like. Then when you hear my signal (demonstrate) **stop and freeze** in any shape you like. Are you ready? Run! Stop and freeze! And run! And stop! Freeze in another shape! And run! (and so forth)

7.

8.

OVER AND UNDER WITH PAPER   (7–8 minutes) *stationary*

Hand out a sheet of construction paper to each child. Then have the children spread out and sit facing you. Call out various body parts adding either "over" or "under" to your call. The children are to put their papers over and under the parts you name, all children in their own way—lying, sitting, standing, kneeling, and so on (see figure 7).

Say:

Spread out and find a place for yourself on the floor and then **sit down with your paper in your hand.** I am going to ask you to **put your paper in different places.** I might say put it *over* a certain place or put it *under* somewhere—so listen carefully first, and then think up a way of doing what I say. Ready? Put your paper **under your arm.** Now put it **over your head.** Put it **under your seat.** Put it **over your knee.** Now put it **under your knee.** How else can you do that? Now put it **over one ear.** Put it **under the other ear.** Put it **under your tummy. Under your elbow. Over your nose. Under your head.** How else can you do that?

Continue this activity for another few minutes, letting the children take turns calling out the different body parts and you adding "over" or "under." Give the instructions in fast succession. The more changes of level and position you give them, the more fun it is. You might end by letting the children put their papers on their backs and then try to move them (by crawling, wriggling, rounding and hollowing their backs, and so on).

JUMPING OVER PUDDLES   (2½–3 minutes) *locomotor*

For a quick change of pace, let the children place their papers on the floor and then jump over them all over the room.

Say:

Put your papers on the floor. Make believe they are puddles and you want to jump over them without getting your feet wet. Start with your own puddle; then continue jumping over as many other puddles as you like.

MAKING BRIDGES   (6–7 minutes) *stationary*

Have the children return to their own "puddles" and make themselves into bridges over the "water." After they have experimented for a while, let them take turns showing the class one bridge of their choice (see figure 8).

Say:

Go back to your own papers. **Can you make a bridge over your puddle?** How else could you do this? You can use an arm, both arms, one leg, or any part of your body you can think of. Now sit down, and one at a time choose your favorite bridge to show us.

MAKING STATUES   (3–4 minutes) *locomotor and stationary*

Let the children walk around in their own pathways among the papers. Then have them stop at your signal and step onto the nearest paper, make a statue, and freeze. Then signal them to continue.

Say:

 Walk around in your own pathways among all the papers. When I give you my signal to stop, **step onto the paper nearest you and make a statue and freeze.** Ready? Walk. (and so on)

STEPPING OVER PARTNERS   (3– 4 minutes) *locomotor*

Collect the papers. Then have the children take partners and go together to one side of the room. The pairs of children should progress across the room by taking turns stepping over each other. Each child should try to make a different low shape each time he or she is to be stepped over (see figure 9).

Say:

 Bring me your papers. Now **choose a partner** and come to this end of the room. (indicate) One person in each couple **make a very low shape** and **let your partner step over you;** then trade places. You could lie in different positions, or crouch down, or kneel bending low, or even sit and stretch your legs out so they can be stepped over. Try to think of a new position every time.

---

6 **Up and Down**
(20– 25 minutes)

Objectives: To explore the directions *up* and *down;* to provide general movement experiences

Special Equipment: Music for "Marionettes" (optional)

RUN! STOP! JUMP UP!   (2– 2½ minutes) *locomotor*

Have the children run freely around the room. At your signal they should stop and jump up into the air. Accentuate each jump with a loud clap or percussive beat. Have the children do 5 to 7 jumps.

Say:

Run around the room wherever you like, and **at my signal stop and jump up into the air.** Are you ready? Run! And jump! And run! (and so on)

UP MOVES   (4– 5 minutes) *stationary*

Have the children lie down and reach up with various parts of their bodies (see figure 10).

Say:

Lie down wherever you are. Now look straight up to the ceiling and point to it. Now **point up with both hands.** Can you point up **with your big toe?** Try pointing up **with the heel** of the other foot. Now **with both legs together**, let's see how high you can reach.

At this point, you might help the children into a shoulder stand. Tell them to roll back first and put their feet behind their heads. Their knees should be bent and close to their ears. Then, with the elbows close to the body, let them support their hips while they raise their legs. Continue the activity by asking the children to reach up with other parts of their bodies.

Use any or all of the following suggestions: the **tummy**; one **arm** and one **leg**; the **seat**; the **toes** (in various ways); and so on. Let them end by making a circle and kicking the legs up as high as possible.

MARIONETTES (6–7 minutes) *locomotor and stationary*

Have the children lie down on the floor. Have them pretend that they are marionettes and that you are pulling strings attached to various parts of them. If the class is small enough, you might touch various places on each of the children; in a larger class, call out the parts the children should raise and then drop as you "let go." Start them out lying on their backs; then have them repeat the activity, starting in another position (on their stomachs, on their sides).

Say:

Make believe you are a marionette—a puppet with many strings attached—and I am pulling you up in different places. Lie flat on your back and wait till I pull you up. **Now I am pulling your arm**; then **I drop it down again**. Now I am pulling your nose up, up, up. Now I drop you down again.

Continue with other body parts: the **chest**; one **knee**; **head** and **body**; both **legs** and both **arms**; the **tummy**; and so on. Try rolling the children over to pull them up by their **seat**. Older children can repeat this with partners, taking turns being the puppeteer who touches the puppet wherever it is to be lifted. End by letting the children be marionettes dancing in their own ways (preferably to music).

UP AND DOWN MOVES (3–5 minutes) *stationary*

Ask the children to stand facing you as you call out various upward and downward moves in fast succession.

Say:

Spread out and stand facing me, and listen carefully. **I am going to call out different upward and downward movements.** Are you ready? **Look** up, **point** down, **reach up** with both hands, **stamp** down, **point** up with your nose, **crouch** down, **shake your head** in an upside-down position, **jump up**, **fall down** and then **jump up** again, **point both feet** up, **point your toes** down. (and so on)

If you wish, you can continue for another short while letting the children come up with ideas, taking one suggestion at a time for all to do.

BE A SEED GROWING UP (5–6 minutes) *stationary and locomotor*

Let the children make believe they are tiny seeds growing and reaching up in different ways, slowly unfolding to grow into specific plants, then being cut off, and finally blowing about in the wind.

Say:

Make believe you are a tiny seed lying warm and comfortable deep in the earth. Now spring is coming and **you start to grow** very, very slowly, rising a bit here, then a bit there, **branching out** as you grow taller and taller, **reaching up** with every part of you. Now you are a beautiful plant enjoying the sunshine. Suddenly **someone comes and cuts you off**, and you fall crumpled up to the ground. Now a **wind picks you up and**

blows you around, and you fly around as you are being blown high and low. Then finally **the wind stops and you sink down**.

Repeat this, first letting the children think of specific plants they would like to grow into. Suggest a few, such as a flower, a tree, or perhaps a vine or ivy growing around a tree trunk. If time permits, let them experience a variety of ideas. In small classes, let the children take turns announcing the plant each wants to be, then letting the class watch their movements. End once more with all moving in unison. If possible, play a soft, slow piece of classical or ballet music as background for this activity.

7 Right, Left, and Sideways
(25–30 minutes)

Objective: To develop the concepts *right, left,* and *sideways*

Special Equipment: An 18- to 24-inch-long paper streamer for each child; music for skipping; orchestral music

SKIP AND TURN WITH A PARTNER (3–4 minutes) *locomotor*

Have the children choose partners and make a circle, with partners standing next to each other. First they can link right elbows and turn around with their partners. Then they can skip forward to music, side by side with their partners, stopping and turning at your signal while the music continues playing.

Say:

 Choose a partner and then stand in one large circle. Now face your partner and **link your right elbows**. (check each couple) Can you **skip around together** in this way? Now stand side by side to go around the circle this way. (indicate the direction by circling your hand) When the music starts, **skip forward side by side.** When I call "right elbow around," stop and face each other and link your right elbows, as before. Then skip around on the spot. Are you ready? Forward, skip. Right elbow around. And again, forward, skip. (and so on)

SIDE MOVES (5–7 minutes) *stationary*

Have the children spread out and stand facing you. Then ask them to make various side movements with different parts of their bodies, first standing, then sitting, and finally lying on the floor (see figure 11). Always remember that your right is the children's left when you face them (and vice versa). Therefore, indicate right and left with your opposite arm so that, from the child's point of view, you will be pointing in the correct direction.

Say:

 Spread out all over the room and **stand facing me. Stretch your arms out** and see if you have enough room at each side without bumping anyone. **Can you reach sideways with your head?** See how far you can reach without falling over. Open your legs a bit wider and see if you can use your head to reach further to the other side. Can you reach from side to side **with your hips**? With **what other parts** of your body can you reach sideways?

12.

Pick one suggestion at a time for all to try in their own ways. You may want to suggest: elbows; knees; shoulders; legs; and so on. After a while let the children try further side moves while sitting down (see figure 12).

Say:

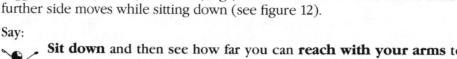

> **Sit down** and then see how far you can **reach with your arms** to each side while you are sitting. Can you **touch your elbows to the floor** on either side? Try **rocking** from side to side.

Have the children try to rock with their legs bent, with their legs straight, and while holding their feet with the soles touching. After a while, have them lie down, cross their legs over, and reach sideways with their legs. Their legs can be straight as well as bent. They also can lie on their side and then kick a leg up high (see figure 13).

SLIDING SIDEWAYS (2–3 minutes) *locomotor*

13.

For a fast change of pace, have the children get up and form a circle, holding hands. Have them slide sideways in unison, stepping out with one leg and closing the gap with the other with a fast little jump. Indicate the direction in which they should go; then clap strong, even beats in a fast rhythm. If you wish, have them change directions once in a while.

Say:

> Make a circle and **stand holding hands**. When I say go, **slide sideways** in this direction, (indicate by circling your hand) stepping out and dragging the other leg quickly closed. Are you ready? Slide and slide and slide and slide. (clapping)

WATCHING THE RIBBON (6–7 minutes) *locomotor and stationary*

To help the children distinguish between left and right, mark their left hands with ribbons: take short pieces of paper streamers and tie one to each child's left wrist. Guiding them with suggestions, let them move their ribbons—first while standing still, then while moving about.

Say:

> **Stand in a large circle and then wave your ribbon** softly from side to side. Let it go high, and then sink down slowly, or circle it around in different places. You could also shake it to different sides. Try going fast . . . and then very slowly. High . . . and then very low. High on one side . . . low on the other. Try turning and watching your ribbon fly overhead.

After a while, let all the children sit down and have them take turns running around the outside of the circle, making their ribbons move in their own ways. After each child has had 2 to 3 turns, you might end by telling them to move any way they like all over the room.

RIGHT AND LEFT STEPS (6–7 minutes) *locomotor and stationary*

Keeping the ribbons still on their wrists, the children should spread out and stand facing you. Then, in fairly quick succession, call out various steps for them to do either to the right or to the left. Clap or use a short drum beat to signal the children to stop one action and to listen for your next call. After you call out each action, pause briefly before giving the direction, so that the children can first think about the move and then carry it out.

Say:

>Spread out all over the room and **stand facing me**. I am going to call out **various steps**. Listen very carefully, because after each one I will tell you whether to go **to your right or to your left. Walk** ... to your right. (stop) **Tiptoe** ... to your left. (stop) **Take 2 giant steps** ... to your right. (and so on)

Continue in a similar way, not always alternating directions.

Use any or all of the following actions: a jump; a full turn; 2 steps and a jump; another full turn to one side and then to the other; 2 jumps; galloping; marching; shuffling the feet; 3 hops and a jump; rolling; walking on the heels; 3 turns; walking on all fours; galloping all the way to one side and then to the other.

CONDUCTING AN ORCHESTRA (2½–3 minutes) *stationary*

Have the children take the ribbons off; then let the children sit down in a group, facing the front. They can pretend to play various instruments in an orchestra, while one child at a time plays conductor (using his or her right hand). You can play any orchestral classical piece, such as a part of a concerto or overture. Change conductor every 30 seconds or so.

Say:

>**Make believe you are playing in an orchestra.** What instruments do you know? (discuss them) Now **choose any instrument** you like, and you can **take turns being the conductor**. Who would like to start?

End by letting everyone get up and freely dance to the music for a minute or so.

8 Open and Close
(20–25 minutes)

Objectives: To explore the concepts *open* and *close;* to experience working with partners

JUMPING JACKS   (1–2 minutes) *stationary*

Have the children spread out and do jumping jacks for a minute or two (8 to 10 jumps in all). Let them jump freely at their own tempo.

Say:

>Do you know what a **jumping jack** is? Stand with your legs together and your arms down at your sides. Now jump to open your legs as you clap your hands above your head. Who wants to demonstrate? Now everybody! Jump! And rest.

WHAT CAN YOU OPEN AND CLOSE?   (4–5 minutes) *stationary*

Have the children sit down in a circle, and ask them what parts of their bodies they can open and close. They will usually start with eyes, mouth, and hands. Take their suggestions, letting them explore the ideas while gradually leading them to incorporate their entire bodies.

14.

Say:

>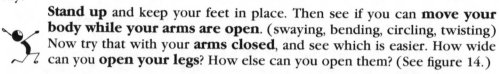
>
> Everyone, **sit down in a circle. What can you open and close?** Can you open your **fingers** wide? Now make a **fist** and quickly open it again. Can you do this in a different direction? Try reaching up as you stretch out your hands with open fingers, then close your fingers and bring your fist down again.

Repeat this a few times and then let them improvise on other suggestions from you. For example, let them open and close their arms, experimenting with various ways to do so: up-down; forward-back; forward-side; back-side; crouching low to make a fist, then kneeling to stretch open hands up above the head; closing the hands low on one side, opening them high on the other; and finally, standing up and moving the body as well as the legs.

Say:

> Stand up and keep your feet in place. Then see if you can **move your body while your arms are open**. (swaying, bending, circling, twisting) Now try that with your **arms closed**, and see which is easier. How wide can you **open your legs**? How else can you open them? (See figure 14.)

Let the children work out ideas on their own while you assist them by making some suggestions.

DOORWAYS WITH PARTNERS   (7–9 minutes) *stationary*

15.

Let the children take partners and then make doorways together, first using their arms, then their legs, and finally other parts of their bodies (see figure 15).

Say:

> **Take a partner** and find a place for yourselves somewhere in the room. How would you **make a doorway together with your arms**? Now find another way.

Let the children look around to see other children's versions; then let them try out a few more ideas.

    You may want to suggest: using both arms; using one arm; standing back to back or sideways; sitting; kneeling, and so on.

    After each couple has had a chance to try out a number of different ideas, let the children choose their favorite doorway. Ask one couple at a time to demonstrate it to the rest of the class, opening and closing it as they do so.

16.

Say:

> Now each couple, **choose your favorite doorway**, and we will look at one couple at a time. How would you open and close your doorway?

After they have all had a turn, let each couple use their legs to make doorways (see figure 16).

Say:

> How would you **make a doorway using your legs**? You could stand, or sit, or even lie down. First think up your idea; then find a way of opening and closing the door.

You might let the children look around to see what others are doing, and perhaps they might try a few of these ideas themselves. If time permits, let each couple demonstrate as before, or have half the class watch as the other half demonstrates. End by letting them make doorways with other parts of their bodies (see figure 17).

PICTURE BOOK   (4–5 minutes) *stationary*

Let the children sit down on the floor and make believe they are picture books or dictionaries, opening and closing their pages (see figure 18).

Say:

> Leave your partners and find a place for yourself on the floor and sit down. **Make believe you are a picture book** or a dictionary with many words and many pages. **How would you open and close your pages?**

In smaller classes you might walk around, stopping near individual children and asking them to freeze for a moment so that you can have a good look. Then they can "close" and try another position as you continue to walk around. In larger classes let the whole group move, while you guide them with your voice.

Say:

> Now everyone make believe **you are standing quietly** on the bookshelf. **I am taking you down** and putting you on my desk, on your side, to open your cover. **I have to turn you around** because your pictures are upside down. Now I open you again and **shuffle through your pages** to look for a special picture (*or* word). Ah, here it is. You **freeze** to let me have a good look, and then **I close you again with a bang!** Now **I put you on your back**, slowly turning the pages, **opening** you wide every time, then **closing you with a bang**. Now I **turn you over, lie you flat** on your face, and then **sit you up** right in front of me. Suddenly there is a draft of air, and it **ruffles through your pages** and makes you **fall over**. You lie flat with your pages blowing about. Then I pick you up, close you, and put you back on my bookshelf.

JUMP TURNS   (2½–3½ minutes) *stationary*

Have the children get up and jump in place, opening and closing their legs as at the beginning of the session, but this time turning themselves a quarter-turn each time they jump.

Say:

> Everyone up on your feet. I would like you to **jump** once again, **opening and closing your legs**. But this time **turn yourself around** as you jump. Start facing the front, then jump to open your arms and legs and close them again. Now each time you open up, you turn a bit to face another wall, then you close again. On your next opening jump, you turn a bit more.

You might end by letting them jump a bit in any way they want, perhaps suggesting they might be jack-in-the boxes: jumping up from a low position, then bobbing around a bit, and ending up in their boxes again.

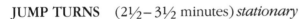

9 Combining Directions
(25–30 minutes)

Objective: To explore the concepts *over, under, through,* and *around*
Special Equipment: 1 small ball (or other object suitable for passing around)

WALKING OVER OBSTACLES   (4–5 minutes) *locomotor*

Let the children walk around freely, making believe they are walking over or through various obstacles, while you direct them with your voice. Pause long enough to let them carry out their ideas for each action.

Say:

> Walk around freely, and listen carefully. Make believe you are **walking in a large park** or wooded area. You **jump over fallen logs** and low shrubs and tree stumps. Now you are getting a bit tired and don't know where you are. So you **climb up a tree** to look out. You **jump down** and **cut through a thick hedge**. It is very muddy there, so you **step over the puddles** very carefully. Then you see an old deserted hut. You **climb over the fence** and then **crawl under some barbed wire** and go into the house. It is full of **cobwebs** and you **duck under** them. You **step over fallen-down planks and rubble**; then you **open a window** and **squeeze yourself through** and **jump down** into the garden. You have to **crawl again under the fence** and **cross a little stream**. First you **balance** yourself **on a narrow beam**, then you **wade across**. It is deeper than you thought, so you have to work hard to get through the water. On the other side there is a **trampoline**, and you **jump on it** for a while. Then you **roll over** in the moss and **rest** under a tree.

MAKING WINDOWS AND LOOKING THROUGH   (6–7 minutes)
locomotor and stationary

Have the children stay on the floor and make windows with different parts of their bodies. Start with simple ideas, using the fingers and hands; then lead them gradually to think up more unusual kinds of windows (see figure 19).

Say:

> Can you **make a window with your fingers**? Try a different one and look through it. What other windows can you make **with your hands**? Now use **your arms** to make a window; it can be above you or below or even behind you. What **other parts** of your body can you make windows with?

Let the children experiment for a while on their own. Encourage them to look around for further ideas. Remind them to try a few in different positions, making some high ones, some very low ones, and so on as they stand, kneel, or even lie in different positions. Point out some of the ideas for everyone to see and perhaps try out. Next let them take partners and have one partner make a series of 2 to 4 windows, which the other partner looks through. Then have them change roles.

Say:

> Take a partner and decide who is number 1 and who is number 2. **Now all ones make a window**—any kind of window—and **let your partner peek through**. Then make a few more windows for your partner to look through. Now change and let the twos make the windows and the ones peek through.

After a few further changes, let the ones once again make windows and the twos look through. This time have the twos go on around the room to peek through all the other windows as well. After a while call for the children to change roles. This is fun: the children walking around have to change their positions, sometimes stretching to peek through a high window, or crouching to see through a very low one. In smaller classes, switch roles 2 to 3 times.

GOING AROUND A PARTNER   (3–5 minutes) *locomotor and stationary*

For a change of pace, let the children move in various ways around their own partners, changing roles each time one goes all the way around.

Say:

> Everyone go back to your partner. Now all ones **walk around your partner**. Now change and twos walk around. Now ones **tiptoe** around your partners. Now twos. Now ones **run** around twice. Now it's the twos' turn. Now **choose your own way** of going around.

After a while ask the ones to go around everyone in the room, all in their own way—sliding, skipping, galloping, and so on—until they are back again with their own partners. Wait until all partners are back together, then ask the twos to do the same thing.

PASSING A BALL   (6–7 minutes) *stationary*

Have the children sit in a circle and hand around a small ball or other suitable object, passing it over, under, or through various parts of their bodies.

Say:

> Make a circle and **sit down**. I would like you to **pass this ball** around, handing it to the child next to you, but passing it over **in your own special way**. You might pass it **over** a certain part of you, or **under**, or perhaps **through** a window, or even **around** yourself. Who would like to start?

Older children can name the position as well as the body part each time they hand the ball along. For example, "I pass it over my elbow," "under my toes," "through my legs," and so on.

DIVIDING THE ROOM   (5–7 minutes) *locomotor*

Divide the room into two separate areas, each for a different type of activity. Then let the children move freely in the area of their own choice. Suggest a few ideas by describing the areas as you point them out.

Say:

> Let's play **make believe**. Pretend that in this area (walk out the perimeter to indicate) **you have a beautiful meadow** where you can romp around, run after butterflies, find frogs and bunnies—or even be one, if you like. And over here (indicate) **you have a bouncy trampoline** where you can jump and bounce as much as you like. Now choose the area you want to go to and play in it in any way you like.

After a while call "change" to let the children try out the other area as well. If you wish, you can divide the room into 3 or 4 areas in the same way.

Other area divisions could be as follows: a toy store and a kitchen; a swimming pool and a playground; a workshop and an amusement park; a zoo/pet store and a skating rink.

2
FUN WITH LETTER SOUNDS

This section offers ear training, which develops greater auditory discrimination as well as concepts relating to sounds (such as long, short, soft, sharp, light, heavy, and so on). It also provides an introduction to simple phrasing.

To take advantage of the step-by-step approach to the elements treated by each lesson, use the activities within each lesson in consecutive order. Once a lesson has been completed, any part of it can be used in conjunction with other lessons in this book. The activities in this section offer wonderful creative outlets that combine movement, rhythm, and sound.

1 Animal Sounds

Objectives: To develop discriminative listening; to introduce sound and movement phrases

ANIMAL SOUNDS   (2½– 3 minutes) *stationary*

Have the children sit in a circle. Name several different animals, and ask the children to imitate the sound each one makes. Focus on one animal at a time.

Say:

Have you ever listened to the different sounds of animals? Can you imitate some of these animals? Who can make a sound like a cat? What does a dog sound like? A little mouse? A cow? A little bird? What other animal sounds do you know?

Take the children's suggestions one at a time, letting all the children try them out. Ask which animals make soft sounds and which make loud sounds.

20.

ANIMAL MOVEMENTS   (5–6 minutes) *locomotor*

Have the children pretend to be the animals whose sounds they have been imitating. Deal with one animal at a time; briefly discuss its movements before having the children imitate it. Ask the children to walk on two legs rather than on four; this allows a wider range of movements.

Say:

 What kind of movements does a cat make? Are they heavy and sharp or quiet and soft? Now **make believe you are a pussycat**, moving about the room. You could be a cartoon cat, walking on 2 feet, but still making the same soft moves as a real cat. Now pretend to be a **dog**. You might be a large dog, growling and digging up a bone. Or you might be a tiny puppy, romping about and wagging your tail. (See figure 20.)

After a while, ask the children to be tiny, squeaking mice, running with tiny steps, sniffing, and nibbling at food. Then have them be horses galloping around, jumping over hurdles or fences, and whinnying. The children could also imitate snakes, frogs, or ducks.

One way to end this activity is for everyone to sit in a circle. Then have the children take turns going around the outside, imitating animals of their choice.

COMBINING TWO SOUNDS   (7–8 minutes) *stationary*

For this activity, the children should remain seated in a circle. Discuss with them the variety of sounds 1 animal can make; then have the children combine 2 different sounds to make up a sound phrase.

Say:

Can a cat make different sounds? (miaow, purr, hiss) Now think of what different sounds a **dog** can make. (bark, growl, whine, howl) How about a **bird**? (short and long chirps, higher and lower sounds) Let's choose an animal and **put 2 of its sounds together** to make a short phrase.

Suggest one idea at a time and let the children take turns repeating the phrase. Have each child repeat the phrase a few times, pausing distinctly before each repeat. Use any or all of the following ideas:

- *Bird:* 2 short and 1 long sound; 3 short and 2 long sounds; or any other combination. (Children could chirp vocally or whistle)
- *Dog:* 1 growl and 1 bark; 1 growl and 2 barks; 3 barks and 1 long growl; a short growl and 2 barks plus 1 long howl.
- *Cat:* 1 purr and 1 miaow; 2 miaows and 1 hiss; 3 miaows and 1 purr.

Then have the children choose 2 sounds to combine.

Say:

 Now **choose your own animal** and **combine 2 of its sounds** into a sound phrase.

Let them think it out for a while. When everyone is ready, have each child present his or her phrase by repeating it 2 or 3 times in a row.

COMBINING TWO SOUNDS WITH TWO ACTIONS   (7–8 minutes)
locomotor

Retaining the sound phrases used in the previous activity, the children can now combine them with movements. A different movement should be devised for each sound in the phrase.

Say:

> Can you **make up a movement to go with each of your 2 sounds**? Get up and try out some movements. When you all are ready, you can take turns showing your movements. Remember, you have 2 sounds so you need 2 movements.

You may want to suggest a few ideas, such as the following:

- *Dog:* Walking carefully and growling, then pouncing or jumping and barking.
- *Cat:* Moving daintily and miaowing, then rolling on its back and purring.
- *Bird:* Hopping 3 times on 1 foot while chirping 3 short notes, then stopping, flapping its wings, and whistling 1 long high note.

When the children are ready, have them sit in a circle and watch as each one takes a turn showing a sound/movement combination.

JOINING A PARTNER   (7–8 minutes) *locomotor*

To end this session, have the children take partners and combine their phrases.

Say:

> **Choose a partner and be 2 animals together.** You can be the same kind of animal (2 dogs, 2 cats, or 2 birds), or 2 different animals (a dog and a cat, or a cat and a bird, and so on). There are 2 ways to do this. You can each use the same sound-and-movement phrase you just made up, and take turns—first one of you moves, then the other one moves, and then you repeat this pattern a few times. Or you can make up a *new* sound-and-movement phrase as you move together. Work out what you want to do. When you are ready, come back to sit in the circle.

When all the children are ready, have one couple at a time perform their phrases. As each couple finishes, discuss the performance of those children. Encourage the children in the audience to watch carefully and listen discriminatively. With older children, you might ask each couple to repeat their sound phrase (without the movements) after they have shown their combination. This will help them grasp the difference between a definite, repeatable phrase and a continuing scenario.

2 Nonvocal Sounds
(30–35 minutes)

Objective: To develop discriminative listening

MAKING NONVOCAL SOUNDS   (5–7 minutes) *stationary*

Have the children sit in a small circle, and ask them to make as many sounds as they can with their hands, their feet, and their mouths—without using their voices.

Say:

What **different sounds** can you make with your **hands**? Who can suggest an idea?

Have the group try out each suggestion. Encourage them to try **clapping, snapping** the fingers, **tapping** on different surfaces, and **rubbing the palms together.** After some exploration, they can combine 2 different hand sounds into a short phrase.

Say:

Can you **combine 2 different sounds** using your hands to make a short sound phrase?

Sound phrase ideas: 2 claps and 1 snap; 3 tapping sounds (on the floor) and 1 clap; rubbing the palms together twice and 3 claps.
    Then have the children try to devise foot sounds.

Say:

Can you make any **sounds with your feet**? You can try out some ideas while you are sitting, and some while you are standing.

Encourage the children to try clapping the feet together (sitting or lying), tapping the toes on the floor, swishing the feet, and stamping. Ask each child to demonstrate an idea.
    Continue by having the children try to make sounds with their mouths.

Say:

Could you use your **mouth**—your tongue, teeth, and lips—to make sounds **without** using your **voice**?

Have the whole group try out each idea.
    Ideas for mouth sounds: clicking the tongue; smacking the lips; or making clipped consonant sounds by pronouncing K, G, P, B, F, S, SH, Z, T, D, H, and R.

COMBINING NONVOCAL SOUNDS   (7–8 minutes) *stationary*

Ask the children to make sound phrases by combining any of the sounds from the preceding activity.

Say:

Now **combine a few sounds** into a short phrase. You can use your hands, your feet, or your mouth, or any combination you like. Make your phrase short enough to remember, so that you can **repeat it for us a few times.**

If necessary, start the children out with a few examples.
    Some ideas for short sound-phrases: 1 clap and 2 stamps; 3 claps and 1 click of the tongue; or a letter sound combined with clapping, tapping, or snapping the fingers (for example, 3 taps on the floor and a long "shhhhhh," or vice versa).
    After all the children have had turns showing their phrases, you might ask some (or all) of them to repeat their ideas for the group to learn.

MOVING WITH SOUND COMBINATIONS   (8–10 minutes) *locomotor*

Ask the children to combine a sound phrase with movements, either using their phrase from the previous activity or making up a new one.

Say:

Everyone up on your feet. I would like you to **add movements to your sound phrases**. Make believe you are a **machine** that makes special sounds as it works—perhaps a **mechanical toy**, a **clock**, or a **robot**. Or you might be a **strange creature**, moving with its own rhythm and sounds. If you like, make up a new sound phrase to put with movements. First think of the thing you want to be; then work it out with sounds and movements; then repeat the same phrase again and again. When you are ready, come and sit down.

When everyone is ready, let each child demonstrate his or her idea. Then ask each one to try it again, but at a different tempo: very fast, then in slow motion.

BUILDING MACHINES   (6–7 minutes) *locomotor*

Have the children "build" a machine by combining their sound and movement phrases into a group composition. Have one child start; then, one by one, add 4 to 6 more children. Then stop them, and start again with another group (see figure 21).

Say:

Let's make a machine by putting several children's phrases together at the same time. You can **repeat** your old movement-and-sound phrase, or you can **make up a new one**. Someone could be low, perhaps lying on the floor puffing and kicking the legs. Someone else might walk forward and backward or around, making their own special sounds. Who would like to start making the machine?

End this lesson by having all the children move freely in unison for a minute or so, each with his or her own sound-and-movement combination.

21.

3 Name Games
(30–35 minutes)

Objectives: To explore word rhythms; to encourage self-expression; to develop body image

MOVE! STOP! MOVE!   (2½–3 minutes) *locomotor*

Let the children move about freely, using their own locomotive ideas. Have them pause every 30 seconds or so and then continue, using a new step. Make the stop signal loud and clear, preferably with a percussion instrument. Let them go through 4 or 5 changes.

Say:

When I say go, move around any way you want to. You can skip or run or march, but listen for this stop signal. (demonstrate) Every time you hear the stop signal, **freeze** for a few seconds, and then **continue with another movement**. Are you ready? Move. (stop) Now move in a different way. (and so on)

STATE YOUR NAME AND MAKE YOUR MOVE   (6–7 minutes) *stationary*

Have the children stand in a circle. One at a time, the children should step forward, call out their names, and make any movement they choose. Give them a few ideas to start out, and demonstrate by introducing yourself first.

Say:

 Make a circle and remain standing. I would like you to introduce yourselves, one at a time. **Call out your name and add a movement to it.** It can be any movement you like. You could jump or skip around or turn. What movement would you like to put with your name?

Offer any or all of the following suggestions: say your name as you walk forward and then bow low; turn around and end with a little jump and a clap; waddle about like a duck and "flap" your elbows as you repeat your name a few times.

Let one child start; then continue in sequence around the circle. This is a good introductory activity for a new school year. It also is useful to repeat this activity, because it allows the children to perfect or change their ideas.

YOUR PARTNER'S NAME AND MOVEMENT   (6–7 minutes) *locomotor and stationary*

Have the children choose partners. Then have them repeat the previous activity, but this time calling out the names of their partners and adding a movement to it.

Say:

 Choose a partner and then **introduce your partner**, adding any movement you think fits his or her name. Make something up, and let me know when you are ready.

Once everyone is ready, call them back into a circle. Let each couple demonstrate their ideas.

SOUND PHRASES WITH NAMES   (7–8 minutes) *stationary*

Have the children sit in a circle and listen as you combine any 2 names into a ditty-like phrase. Have the children first repeat the phrase after you a number of times. Then have them make up their own combinations.

Say:

Let's **combine 2 names to make a sound phrase**. Which names shall I start with? (choose 2 of the children's names) Listen and repeat it after me.

22.

Ideas for name phrases (accent the syllables as shown): Tom and **An**dy (repeat several times); or Tom and **An**dy, **An**dy and Tom; or **Tom**, **Tom**, Andy and **Tom**; or **An**dy, **An**dy, **An**dy and **Tom**.

Have the children clap the rhythm while they repeat the phrases along with you. After a while, have the children work in pairs to make name phrases by combining their names.

Say:

Take a partner and then **make up a rhythmic phrase** using both of your names.

Let the children work out the phrases on their own; then have each couple demonstrate their ideas.

NAME DANCE WITH PARTNERS   (8–10 minutes) *locomotor*

Have the partners in the previous activity work remain partners to make up name dances.

Say:

 Get up. **With your partner**, make up a little dance together — an introduction dance. **Combine your names** to make a phrase and **add movements** to make a short dance. Spread out and decide how you are going to do it. When you are ready, come and sit down again in the circle.

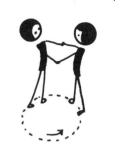

Usually, the children will come up with their own ideas readily enough. However, if they need assistance, use any or all of the following ideas:

1. Skip forward side by side, with or without holding hands, while repeating both names a number of times (for example, "Jane and Dinah"). Then both stop, and first one jumps into the air calling her name (Dinah!), then the other does the same ("and Jane!") (see figure 22).
2. Stand face to face, holding both hands. Then with sliding sideways steps, revolve in a little circle on the spot while repeating their names 3 or 4 times (for example, "Elizabeth and Janie"). Then both stop and stamp 3 times (see figure 23).
3. Stand face to face clapping hands, as in Pat-a-Cake (alternately clapping their own hands and their partner's palms), while calling out both names 3 times (for example, "Tom and Andy"). Then both stop, and first one child turns around calling out his or her name ("Andy"), then the other does the same ("and Tom") (see figure 24).
4. Bow or curtsy, one after the other while saying their names (for example, "My name is Dinah. And my name is John"), then linking right elbows and skipping around on the spot. They can repeat this activity, perhaps now calling out their names in reverse order and then linking their left elbows to skip around (see figure 25).

4 Long and Short
(25–30 minutes)

Objective: To explore time factors

LONG AND SHORT STEPS (3½–4 minutes) *locomotor*

Have the children walk about, changing tempo to match your calls. Use a drum beat or loud clap every time before calling a change.

Say:

 Walk around wherever you like, but **listen** carefully. I am going to call out different ways of walking. Are you ready? Walk **normally**. (signal) Walk very **fast**. (signal) Walk very, very **slowly**. (signal) Walk with **pauses**: take a few steps, then pause for a few seconds, and continue walking. Walk. (signal) And pause. And walk. (and so on)

Repeat this last sequence 4 or 5 times, calling out the pauses at varying intervals. After a while, if you wish, you can let the children decide when to pause instead of you giving them a signal. Then have them continue with the following variations: walking with **long steps**; walking with **short steps**; combining **long and short steps** in any way they like.

End this activity by having the whole class cross from one side of the room to the other — first with short jumps (there and back), and then with very long jumps (with a run in between).

Say:

Everyone, **come to this end of the room**. When I say go, **go across the room**, making many little **short jumps**. When you get to the other side, stop and wait. Now **run and leap** to make as long a step as you can. Ready? Run. And leap!

LONG AND SHORT SOUNDS (4–5 minutes) *stationary*

Have the children sit in a circle. They will be exploring long and short sounds, first by making long sounds, then by listening for long and short sounds in names.

Say:

Sit down in a circle. **Take a deep breath** and **slowly breathe out**. Take a long time breathing out. Try that once again, and **make a soft "sssss"** as you breathe out, so that I can hear you make a really long sound.

Repeat this a few times; then have the children make an "ooooo" sound a few times. Finally, have them breathe out with many short breaths, making fast "sh" sounds like a train. End this activity by saying some names aloud and asking the children to distinguish between long and short parts of the names.

26.

Say:

Listen as I call out some **names**, and tell me which part of the name has a **long sound** and which part has a **short sound**.

The following names work well in this activity: Mary; Doreen; Serena; Norman; Eileen. Repeat each name a number of times to give the children a chance to analyze it. End by letting them find the long and short parts of their own names.

LONG AND SHORT MOVES (6–7 minutes) *stationary*

Have the children stand in a large circle. Ask them first to make long moves, then short moves, using different parts of their bodies (see figure 26).

Say:

How could you **make a long movement with your arm**? Stand up and try out different ideas. You could draw a long line by slowly going up and down, or from side to side, all the way across as far as you can reach. Or you could make a slow, long line that goes in a circle all around you. Now use your other arm and make some more long lines. They can be straight, or wavy, or curve in and out.

After a while, have the children try making short, fast moves.

Say:

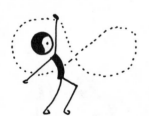
Now let's make **short, fast moves**. What short movements could you do with your **head**? (nod, shake, tilt, drop, lift, turn) Now try some with your **shoulders**. With your **elbows**. How could you make short, fast movements with your **hands**? (shaking them, pushing, pulling, punching, waving, and so on) How could you make short moves with your **body**? (wriggling, pushing the hips from side to side, leaning, and so on). Now **sit down**, and let's find different long and short movements for your **legs**.

If the children are older, have them make different leg moves and then ask them whether the movements are long or short. If the children are younger, give them both long and short leg movements as they sit.

Ideas for long movements: drawing circles, lines, or curves in the air; slowly stretching a leg while lying on the back or on the side; crossing the leg over from one side to the other while lying on the back; making figure 8s, and so on.

Ideas for short movements: tapping the toes; short kicks; little fast circles; crisscrossing the legs in the air at a fast tempo; stamping.

End this activity by having the children make short, bouncing little jumps in place.

RUBBER BAND (3–3½ minutes) *stationary*

Have the children lie down and make believe they are rubber bands being pulled in different places and toward various directions, snapping back each time. You may want to use a drum beat or a loud clap to signal snapping back.

Say:

> **Make believe you are a rubber band** lying curled up on my desk. Now I stretch you in different places. First I pull you on one side and watch you grow longer and longer. Then I let you go and you snap back! Then I pull you somewhere else and make you long . . . and let you snap back! Now **you** decide which different parts of you are being pulled each time. I might pull your tummy or your leg . . . and then you snap back! Then I may pull your elbow, and you grow longer and wider . . . then you snap back! And I stretch you again at another part . . . and you snap back! And stretch . . . and snap back! And stretch. (and so on)

Continue for another minute or so; then go on to the next activity.

CHEWING GUM (3–3½ minutes) *stationary*

Have the children pretend to be pieces of chewing gum. Direct them as in the previous activity, calling out actions slowly, and pausing long enough for them to make their moves.

Say:

> **Make believe you are a piece of chewing gum.** First you are in a package, all stiff and wrapped up. Now someone unwraps you and puts you into his mouth, and he starts to chew. You feel yourself turned over and over, and you become softer and softer. Now you are a ball of gum. Then he pulls you and stretches you, making you longer and longer. Then he rolls you together again. Then he stretches you in another way, and squashes you together into a little ball. (repeat a few more times) Then he tosses you and turns you, and suddenly he spits you out! You jump and fall to the ground, and there you lie, stuck in a funny shape.

COMBINING SOUNDS AND MOVEMENTS (6–7 minutes) *locomotor*

Ask the children to think of a short sound phrase that combines a short sound and a long sound. Then have them move about freely, alternating long and short moves to accompany their sounds.

Say:

> Think of **a long sound and a short sound** and **put them together.** For example, a long "huuuu" and a short "ha"! Or a long "miaow" and a short "sssss"! Or perhaps a long howl and then a few short yips like "ee, ee, ee"! When you have your 2 sounds, move about. **Make yourself long** to go with your long sound, and then snap together to **become short** when you

make your short sound. Continue to move, growing long and short in many different ways, but use the same long and short sounds the whole time.

After the children have experimented for a while, you might let half the class watch while the other half moves. Then reverse.

Heavy and Light 5
(25–30 minutes)

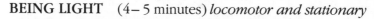

Objective: To explore the concept of force
Special Equipment: A drum or similar instrument; ballet music (optional)

BEING HEAVY   (3–4 minutes) *locomotor*

Ask the children to move freely, pretending to be heavy animals or other beings, as you guide them with your voice.

Say:

> Make believe you are **a great big heavy bear** stomping in the woods. Every step you take is heavy; your whole body feels heavy as you move. You feel your paws sink down into the soft ground with every step. Sometimes there is a fallen tree or stump blocking your path, and you jump over it in your clumsy way. Then you sit back and rest. But a fly is bothering you, and you try to swat it away with your heavy paw. Then you get up and run softly, but heavily, through the deep woods.

Ask the children what other heavy animals they know of; let them move accordingly for a few minutes. They may suggest elephants, walruses, lions after a heavy meal, and so on. Next let them be giants, and finally monsters.

Say:

> Now **make believe you are a giant**, but you are **a very sleepy giant**. You are big and heavy, but so sleepy that you can barely lift your feet. So you shuffle along, trying to push the branches aside with your heavy arms, and you flop with every step you take. Now be **a big heavy monster** scaring everyone around you.

BEING LIGHT   (4–5 minutes) *locomotor and stationary*

Have the children sit down around you. Ask them to try breathing heavily and then lightly, making heavy or light sounds. Then ask them to make light sounds using their hands. Finally, ask them to move as if they were snowflakes.

Say:

> Sit down in a circle. Now breathe a **long heavy breath**. Now try a **light short breath**. Can you **make a light sound** with your hands? (tapping, rubbing or swishing palms, and so on) What **objects** do you know of that are light?

Have the children list as many as they can (paper, balloons, raindrops, leaves, and so on). Then ask them to be snowflakes, guiding them with your voice.

Say:

Make believe you are a snowflake, softly floating through the air. The wind sweeps you **up and down**, and **swirls and turns you around**. On and on you swirl. Then, gently and lightly, you **settle down** on a branch of a tree. For a while you lie there, **gently rocking** to and fro with your branch. Then another gust of wind **sweeps you up** and blows you around again. Once more you **float and swirl**, until finally you **lightly fall** down to the ground.

If you wish to continue (now or at another time), let the children be other light things. They might be a **balloon** bouncing and floating softly, slowly turning as it moves; or a **leaf**, first swaying on a branch, then being torn away and swirling in gusts, finally gently floating down; or **mist** rising from a lake and slowly covering the countryside, reaching with long, soft moves as it spreads out and moves along.

LIGHT AND HEAVY SOUNDS   (4–5 minutes) *locomotor*

Using a drum (or other instrument), make light and heavy sound sequences, letting the children move in their own ways to the rhythm.

Say:

Spread out all over the room. I want you to **listen** very carefully, for I am going to give you **different beats to move to**. You can move any way you like, but first **listen to whether the sound is light or heavy**. Then make up a movement that goes with it. Are you ready? Listen.

Ideas for sound phrases follow. (Dots are short light sounds, dashes are long and heavy.) A light, even beat: . . . .; a fast light beat: . . . .; a light double beat: . . . .; a heavy double beat (fast): -- -- -- -- --; 3 heavy beats and a pause (slow): --- --- --- ---; 3 light and 1 heavy beat . . . - . . . -

Repeat each phrase 8 to 10 times to give the children a chance to listen, think, and try out various ideas until they find one with which they are comfortable.

Be sure to keep the rhythm even, including the length of the pauses between the phrases. It might help you to count quietly to yourself during long pauses (for example, 3 heavy beats and a pause, with 3 counts for the pause).

FAIRY AND TEDDY BEAR   (7–8 minutes) *locomotor*

Have the children work in pairs: one should be number 1, the other should be number 2. To start, let all ones be teddy bears and let all twos be fairies bringing the teddy bears to life.

Say:

Choose a partner and decide who will be number 1 and who will be number 2. Then find a space for yourselves in the room. Now all ones, make believe you are **teddy bears in a toy store**. You are soft and cuddly, but you are stiff and you sit quietly in your corner. All twos, you are **fairies**. You come softly in at midnight with light dainty steps, and with your wand you bring the teddy bears to life. You touch them gently here and there and show them how to move. Finally you both dance together. The fairies dance very lightly, and the teddy bears dance heavily and clumsily, but very happy to be moving.

All teddy bears, get into your positions. You can be sitting, or lying, or standing up if you wish. All fairies, move further away so that you can come floating in. Everybody move!

If possible, play music as they move, either dainty ballet music or a light classical piece. After a while, have the partners change roles. Repeat this a few times, each time having them start from their original places.

Ideas for variations: fairies and dragons; giants and elves; ballerinas and dancing bears; tortoises and hares.

FLOATING IN THE UNIVERSE   (5–7 minutes) *locomotor*

Ask the children to move about freely, making believe they are floating in the universe without weight or force, in any shape they wish. When they get close to one another they are to react in some way and change direction, level, speed, or even shape. First describe the situation. Then let them move on their own, adding their own sounds as they move.

Say:

> **Make believe you are a star or a planet floating somewhere in space.** You have **no weight or strength** but you can feel magnetic currents that sometimes make you move faster and sometimes make you move slower. Whenever you get close to another planet, react in some way. You might shoot off in another direction, or perhaps bounce off and twirl around, changing your shape and perhaps your level. Then float on again at your own speed, sailing through the vast universe. Get into your positions; make any shape you like. Everybody ready? Slowly move. You can add your own strange sounds as you move along.

After a while let half the class sit and watch the others move, then change over. Repeat this a few times so the children can incorporate new ideas. Suggest that their shapes might vary from round to square to lopsided. Perhaps they might quiver occasionally, or plop down, or spiral up and down before floating on again weightlessly.

Letter Sounds
(25–30 minutes) 6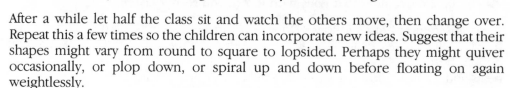

Objective: To develop auditory, vocabulary, and spelling skills

MOVING TO CONSONANT SOUNDS   (3–5 minutes) *locomotor*

Choose one consonant or a consonant blend and repeat it many times in one specific way while the children listen and move freely to it. Repeat each sequence 15 to 20 times. Then change to another sound, repeating it in the same way. When changing sounds, also change the intonation, speed, or intensity of your voice. This will give the children a new impetus for doing movements.

Say:

> Today I would like you to **listen and move to letter sounds**. Some of the letters have quiet sounds, so you have to listen very carefully. You can move in any way you like. You can even stand or lie on the floor if you feel like it. **Move in whatever way you think fits the sound.** Are you ready? Listen.

Use any or all of the following suggestions. (Pronounce the sound only, not the letter name.)

- (slowly, softly): /b/ /b/ /b/ /b/ /b/ /b/ /b/ (and so forth)
- (faster): /b/ /b/ /b/ /b/ /b/ /b/ /b/ /b/ (and so forth)
- (slow and heavy): /k/ /k/ /k/ /k/ /k/ /k/ (and so forth)
- (slow with a heavy accent): /k/ /k/ /*k*/ /k/ /k/ /*k*/ /k/ /k/ /*k*/ (and so forth)
- (very softly and quietly): /st/ /st/ /st/ /st/ /st/ /st/ (and so forth)
- (strong with longer pauses): /p/ /p/ /p/ /p/ /p/ (and so forth)
- (combining soft and strong): /d/ /d/ /*t*/ /d/ /d/ /*t*/ (and so forth)

MOVE AND FREEZE GAME   (7–8 minutes) *locomotor and stationary*

Get a piece of paper and pencil and ask the children to sit around you. Choose a consonant, pronounce its sound, and have the children list as many words as they can that start with that sound. Write down the words they call out. Then have the children move freely as you call out one word at a time from the list, repeating it many times. Now and again sneak in a word that starts with a different sound, repeating it exactly the same way. Tell the children to keep moving as long as the word you are calling starts with the original letter sound, but to freeze when you call a word with a different initial sound. If you use up the children's suggestions, add more words to the list. The sequence is not important, but vary the speed, force, and intonation of each sequence as much as possible. Repeating each word for a prolonged time (15 to 20 times or more) allows the children to relax and enjoy the movements.

Say:

> Come and sit close to me. Here is a letter sound: (for example) /b/. What words can you think of that start with this sound? (list them) Now everyone, up on your feet. **I am going to call out one word at a time from our list, and you move to it any way you wish.** But you have to listen very carefully. Keep moving as long as I call out a word that starts with the /b/ sound. **When I call out a word that starts with a different sound, freeze.** So you have to listen carefully all the time. Are you ready?

You may want to use the following sequence, which illustrates the method described above.

- (softly): boat boat boat boat boat boat (and so forth)
- (fast and high): bunny bunny bunny bunny bunny bunny (and so forth)
- (heavy and low): bear bear bear bear bear (and so forth)
- (light and soft): butterfly butterfly butterfly butterfly (and so forth)
- (normal): snow snow snow snow snow snow (repeat until all the children are "frozen")
- (normal): boy boy boy boy boy (and so forth)
- (fast): chipmunk chipmunk chipmunk chipmunk (and so forth)
- (normal): ball ball ball ball ball (and so forth)

This activity can be adapted for a variety of studies. For example:

1. To distinguish one specific vowel sound, have the children move to any word with that sound and freeze to words without it. You can have them do the same thing for consonants or letter blends.
2. For syllable counting, have the children move to words with two (or more) syllables (for example), and freeze for one-syllable words.
3. For spelling purposes, use only one specific sound or letter blend. List the words on the chalkboard and contrast them with words of different sounds. This gives the children a chance to absorb and memorize one specific word

list. For example, for the *ow* sound (as in *how*), move to words such as *now, how, cow, bow,* and *howl,* and freeze to words without an *ow* sound, such as *tree, car, turn,* and *pool.*

WORD INTERPRETATIONS   (7–8 minutes) *locomotor and stationary*

Using the word list from the previous activity (or a new one, if you prefer), call out one word at a time. This time, however, call the word only once. The children are to devise movements to interpret each word you call. The sequence is not important, but try to include all the children's words; they will enjoy using their own ideas. Change words every 40 to 60 seconds.

Say:

> Everybody, come here and listen. I am going to call out the words from our list again, but this time **when I call out a word, act it out** any way you wish. For example, I might say **ball**! Then you could make believe you are playing with a ball, throwing it, kicking it, and making it bounce. Or I might call **bus**! You might be the driver and drive a bus around, or you might run after it and jump aboard and rattle along with it. You might even be the engine of the bus, puffing and working hard to make it move. All right? Spread out and listen.

If some children occasionally draw a blank with a word (which is rare), suggest that they use an association. For example, if you call *blue,* they might think of the sky and then be a cloud floating or a bird, and so forth.

GUESS THE WORD   (6–8 minutes) *locomotor and stationary*

Have the children sit down in a large circle. Each child takes a turn choosing and acting out a word from the preceding list while the others try to guess the word.

Say:

> Make a circle and sit down. Now **choose your own word** with our special sound for today, (for example, /b/) and **act it out. The rest of us are going to guess your word** and what you are doing. Who would like to start?

Word Rhythms
(30–35 minutes) 7

Objectives: To develop auditory skills; to explore rhythms in syllables and words

CLAP A WORD   (4–5 minutes) *stationary*

Have the children sit in a circle. Ask them first to name, then to clap in rhythm, the syllables of the names of various objects in the room. Let them clap each word several times before going on to a new word.

Say:

> Look around the room and **name a few of the objects you see**. Now let's take one of these words. (for example, *window*) Listen to the word as I say it. (repeat it a few times) Can you **clap out the rhythm**? Let's try it together.

Say the word as you clap out the syllables in rhythm and let the children follow you, repeating the word several times. Then have them take turns trying it out alone. Continue in a similar way with other words such as *writing desk* and *blackboard*. After a while, let the children combine 2 or more words into a short phrase, clapping it out in a similar way.

Say:

 Let's **combine a few words**. Listen first and then see if you can **clap out the rhythm** as I say it.

Ideas for phrases: pen and *pen*cil; blackboard and *chalk;* colored *pa*per; *blue* sneakers, *red* sneakers; and so forth. (Accents are indicated.) Lead the class, repeating each phrase many times before starting a new one. Let the children clap and say each phrase along with you first; then let individuals try on their own.

CLAP A SENTENCE (5–7 minutes) *stationary*

Continue the previous activity by letting the children figure out and then clap the rhythms of short sentences, clapping each syllable (the claps should be louder for accented syllables). Start them out with your suggestions; then let them find their own rhythms.

Say:

 Now let me give you a few sentences. First **listen to the rhythm and the accents**, and then try to **clap it out**.

Ideas for sentences (the accents are indicated): **rain** is **fall**ing; **rain** is **fall**ing, let's go **in**; I'm **go**ing to a **par**ty, **yay**, **yay**, **yay**; **we** play **ball** in the **gar**den; **we** were **play**ing **all** day **long**; we had **ice** cream and **cake**.

MOVE WITH THE RHYTHM (8–10 minutes) *locomotor*

Next have the children make up movement phrases to go with the sentences. Call out one sentence at a time, saying it and clapping it out simultaneously while the children make up movements to go with it. Repeat it many times (20 to 25 times, or for about 1½ to 2 minutes) to give the children a chance to experiment with, improve, and enjoy their movement variations. Observe the children; ask a few to demonstrate their ideas. Call the class's attention to the good points, such as an accent well taken or a particularly interesting movement sequence or interpretation. After a while, use a different sentence, perhaps one suggested by a child. Say the sentences rather slowly, pausing between repetitions. This allows the children to enlarge their range of movements and gives them a chance to think.

Say:

Let me give you **one sentence**. Listen to the rhythm, then get up and **move with it**. **Show me the accents** with your movements. Find one special movement phrase and keep repeating it as I repeat the sentence and clap it out for you. You might show your accents by going high and low, or becoming wide and narrow, or perhaps by giving a little jump. Try out many ideas until you find something you like. Are you ready? Listen.

Choose a sentence suggested in the previous activity and repeat it until all the children are ready. Continue with a few more sentences and, if time permits, let the children take turns showing their movements.

SOUND ORCHESTRA   (5– 6 minutes) *stationary*

Let the children once again sit down in a circle; then give them different words to repeat. Let them repeat these words in unison first; then after a while, divide the class into groups and give each group a different word. Then direct them as an orchestra conductor would. Point to the different groups in turn, letting them vary the intensity of their sounds or stopping them. Occasionally, some or all groups speak in unison. Make the groups by arbitrarily dividing the circle into sections.

Say:

> Everybody, come and sit in a large circle. We are going to **make a sound orchestra and listen to the sounds of different words.** No clapping. Let me give you a word and you all repeat it after me.

Let the children repeat each word in unison a number of times before going to the next one.

It is best if all the words are chosen from the same general category, such as birds, flowers, holidays, nature, and so on. Examples of weather words might be as follows: sunshine, sunshine, sunshine, sunshine; rain, rain, rain; hurricane, hurricane, hurricane, hurricane; winnnnnd, winnnnnd, winnnnnd, winnnnnd.

Similarly with, for example, *flowers:* forget-me-nots, lilies, violets, buttercups, and so on; *animals:* butterflies, frogs, squirrels, foxes, eagles, and so on.

Words can also be combined to make interesting sound and rhythm combinations, such as: "trick and *treat*," "witches and *broom*sticks," "*pump*kin pie," "*butt*ercups and *dai*sies," and so on.

27.

AN ORCHESTRA OF SOUND AND MOVEMENT   (8– 10 minutes) *locomotor and stationary*

Continue as in the previous activity, adding simple movements for those in each group to do as they say their respective word. The children can be stationary for these movements, but each group could be in a different posture for variety (standing, kneeling, sitting), and perhaps one group could be moving around as well. Let the children make suggestions for movements; help them choose contrasting moves for each group.

28.

Say:

> **Let us find a movement for each of these words.** Let's take one word at a time. How would you move to **sunshine**? Spread out a bit to try things out. You can move kneeling, sitting, or standing in place, so that you can do the movement as a group later on.

After selecting one movement sequence for each group, have the children come back again to their places. Conduct the children as before, having them speak and stop according to your directions. End with all groups speaking and moving at once, like a large chorus, each with their own roles. If time permits, let the groups change roles, so that children can experience additional parts.

Here are some suggestions for simple movements:

29.

- *Sunshine:* Slowly raise the arms overhead, open them wide to describe a large circle, and slowly lower them again while in a sitting position (see figure 27).
- *Rain:* Raise and lower the arms and the body from a kneeling position (see figure 28).
- *Wind:* Stand and swing the arms and the body from side to side, or just move the arms about in a swaying motion. This group should spread out enough to avoid hitting one another (see figure 29).

- *Hurricane:* Either rise, turn and sink down continuously, or move about and around the other groups, turning and swaying. In this case, however, have the children choose a leader to follow so that you can conduct the group by signalling only one child (see figure 30).

3
FUN WITH LETTER SHAPES

This section deals with letter shapes in both two-dimensional and three-dimensional forms. These shapes are explored through three basic activities: drawing the letters in the air, walking out pathways in the shapes of letters, and forming letter shapes with the body. In this section, all three activities are combined in the following progression: simple straight-letter forms; curved forms; letters that use combinations of straight and curved lines. First use the lessons in this section in consecutive order; later, you can combine various activities in your own way.

Walking out simple letter shapes provides a good warm-up, and drawing letters in the air can offer an excellent body workout, if proper guidance is given.

1 The Straight Line and the Letter *I*
(25–30 minutes)

Objective: To develop conceptual images of the straight line and the letter *I*

FIND AN EMPTY SPOT AND GO THERE   (3–4 minutes) *locomotor*

Have the children spread out in the room and stand facing you. Then ask them to focus on an empty spot somewhere on the floor, and on your signal, to go there, first using a movement you suggest, then using movements they think of themselves. Use a percussive beat to signal a stop after each action, and to alert the children to your next challenge.

Say:

> Spread out all over the room and stand facing me. Now **look at an empty spot** somewhere on the floor. The spot can be near you or ahead of you, or anywhere at all. Has everyone found an empty spot? Wait for my signal to

go, and then **run toward it**. Ready? Run! (stop) Now find another empty spot, somewhere else. This time when I signal go, **sneak** toward it very carefully. Ready? Go! (stop) Find another empty spot, and **hop** to it. Keep your eyes glued to your spot while you are moving. Now look for another empty spot. **How else** could you get there? Who has a good idea?

Choose one movement at a time from the children's suggestions. If you like, suggest a few of your own in between.

Ways to move: walking on **tiptoes**; **jumping** like a frog; **walking backward**; **sliding** on seats; **step-hopping**; **galloping**; **rolling**. End this activity by letting each child choose a spot and then think of a movement. Then have all the children travel simultaneously to their spots in their different ways. However, do this only once, or else it may become increasingly frenetic.

BE A STRAIGHT LINE (4–5 minutes) *stationary*

Let the children remain standing wherever they are. Briefly discuss the straight line as the shortest distance between two spots. Then ask the children to make themselves straight, first using the whole body, then using body parts (see figure 31).

Say:

Stand very straight. Can you **make yourself straight** in another way? You can be in any position you like.

The most likely variations will be **standing** with arms straight up or down, and **lying** in different positions (on the side, back, or face) with the arms extended or clamped to the sides, perhaps with the toes pointed. Point out different positions as the children think of them, and encourage them to try out one another's ideas. Then go on to make straight lines with parts of the body.

Say:

What part of your body can you make straight? (arms, legs, back) **Now show me different straight lines you can make using different parts of your body.** For example, you could make one long line going from your hand all the way down to your foot, in different directions. You could be kneeling, sitting, leaning, or standing. How many different ways can you make a straight line?

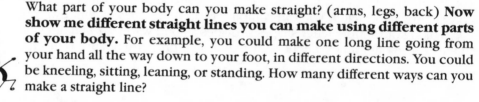

Demonstrate a few ideas to start them out; then let each child (or a few) show one idea. After a while have them all take one position and call out "change" at 10-second intervals for 1 or 2 minutes. Occasionally, point out interesting poses, encouraging the children and helping them try out new ideas as they move.

DRAWING STRAIGHT LINES (4–5 minutes) *stationary*

Have the children stand in their places or in a circle, and let them draw straight lines in the air as many different ways as possible, using different parts of their body. These lines can be vertical, diagonal, or horizontal, on various levels, going in different directions. Encourage the children to make each line as long as possible to achieve maximum body action.

Say:

Everyone up on your feet (*or* come into a circle)! I would like you to **draw a long straight line in front of you**. Now draw one **on one of your sides**; now on your **other side**. Can you draw one **behind you**?

Who can suggest another straight line in **a different place** that everyone can draw? Lines can go up and down, or from side to side, and in different places going in different directions, just as long as they're straight.

After a while have the children **change hands**; then have them **sit down** and use their **hands**, and then their **legs**. End this activity by letting them stand to draw a few more lines with their **heads**. (See figure 32.)

THE LETTER *I*   (4–5 minutes) *stationary*

Write the letter *I* on the chalkboard; then ask the children to shape the letter with their bodies, first alone, then with a partner (see figure 33).

Say:

Can you **shape an *I* with your body**? How else can you do that? You could make believe you are lying inside the pages of a book. The book might even be upside down. Now **take a partner**, and **try out some ideas** together.

THE DOT THE *I* GAME   (3–4 minutes) *locomotor*

Have each set of partners shape a lowercase *i*, one lying flat and the other being the dot. When all are in their positions have the dots quickly change places on your signal, each one finding another *i* to dot. Repeat this 4 or 5 times and then have the dots and the *i*s change roles (see figure 34).

Say:

All partners, **make a lowercase *i***. One of you will be the letter, and the other will be the dot. (let them get into position) Now **all dots**, listen carefully: when I say change, get up and run to **find another *i*** to dot. I might ask you to change a few times, so keep listening. Are all the dots ready? Change! Change again! And change! (and so on)

WORDS STARTING WITH *I*   (7–8 minutes) *locomotor and stationary*

Start by asking the children to list words starting with the letter *I*. Write their suggestions on the chalkboard. Then let them interpret several of the words as you guide them with your own suggestions.

Say:

Let's play make-believe using words that start with an *I*. (list words; *island,* for example) **Make believe there is an island at the other end of this room**, surrounded by water. Everyone come to this end of the room and **try to reach the island in your own way**. You could swim across, or you could wade through the deep water, or you could go by boat, rowing or sailing across and then pulling your boat ashore. Choose your own way to reach the island.

Watch for interesting ideas during the first effort. Then have one or more children demonstrate their versions to the rest of the class. Go through the scenario a few more times so that the children can try out new ideas. Continue in a similar way with interpretations of other words, guiding the children along. Possible *I* words: **icicle**, hanging stiff and straight from a tree, slowly melting as the sun comes out, getting shorter, dripping, and finally falling down onto the ground; **ice cream**, standing frozen on a plate, slowly being eaten and melting; finally, **ink** splashing into **ink spots**.

Say:

Now **make believe you are ink** in a bottle and I am shaking the bottle. Move round and round, wriggling or running, sloshing and jerking as **I shake you**. Now you slosh out of the bottle and you are an **ink spot splashing to the floor in a funny shape**.

Repeat a few times, having the children get up to move as you "shake" them, then having them fall to the floor in funny shapes. Use a percussive beat to emphasize each fall.

The Round Line, the Circle, and the Letter *O*
(30–35 minutes)

2

Objective: To develop conceptual images of the circle and the letter *O*
Special Equipment: Record of orchestral music (classical)

35.

BE A BROOK   (2½–3 minutes) *locomotor*

Let the children run around freely in curving and circular paths, pretending to be brooks as you guide them with your voice.

Say:

Make believe you are a little brook running and circling around in the forest. You curve your way through the moss, **weaving in and out** around the trees. Sometimes you **jump over stones** that are in your path. Sometimes you **make a few circles** around them; then you run on again, **jumping, bubbling,** curving your way in and out and around. Sometimes you go **faster,** and sometimes you **slow down**, almost standing still before you bubble on again and jump along your way.

ROUND LINE, CIRCLE, AND LETTER *O*   (8–10 minutes) *stationary*

Have the children stand in a circle and shape round lines with their arms and bodies. Then have them sit down and draw circles in the air with different parts of their bodies. You might first briefly discuss the round-line pathways they used in the preceding activity, where they were pretending to be brooks (see figures 35 and 36).

Say:

What kind of pathway does a brook have? Is it straight or rounded? Can you **shape a round line with your arms**? How else can you do this? Now make a round line **with your back**.

Have the children sit down and, as best they can, make circles with different body parts.

Say:

Sit down, and let's see how many different circles we can make. Can you **make a circle with your head**? Now try making one **with your shoulders**. Who can think of **another part** to make a circle with?

Take one suggestion at a time and have all the children try it. If necessary, provide them with ideas such as the following: **toes; elbows; torso; nose; 1 finger; hand; foot; leg; both legs together;** and so on. After a while have them stand and try making larger "circles" using **the whole body**.

End this activity by having the children write the letter *O* in as many different ways as possible (see figure 37).

Say:

> I would like you to **write the letter *O* in different places** around you. **Whenever I call "change," find a new place for the letter *O*.** It can be high up, low down, underneath you, or facing different directions. It can be standing up, lying flat, and all different sizes. Are you ready? Draw an *O*. Change! And change! (go on for as many as 10 to 15 changes)

WALK! STOP! SKIP OUT A CIRCLE   (2½–3 minutes) *locomotor*

For a fast change of pace, have the children walk around at random, stop at your signal, skip out a small circle, and continue walking to a new spot. Use a percussion instrument to make a clear stop signal. Repeat 8 to 10 times.

Say:

> Spread out and **find a place for yourself** somewhere in the room. Now make believe there is a small **circle** drawn around the spot where you stand, and **skip around it**. Now **walk** to another place in the room. Stop, and **skip a circle** there. The circle can be large or small. Now walk. Stop. And skip out your new circle. Walk. Find another spot. Stop. And skip a circle. (and so on)

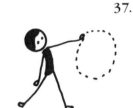

THE MOVE AND FREEZE GAME   (5–6 minutes) *locomotor*

This activity is similar to the Move and Freeze game on page 33. This time, let the children move to words that contain a long **O** sound, as in **go**, and have them freeze to all other sounds. Start by having them list as many words as they can think of that have the long **O** sound. Then call out each word, repeating it 10 to 15 times or so as they move.

Say:

> How many words do you know that have an *O* sound inside them, like the word **go**? (list the words on the chalkboard) Now get up and **move about in any way you like. When I say a word with the long *O* sound**, you can move; when I say a word with a **different sound**, you must **freeze**. Are you ready?

A possible word sequence: slow, slow, slow, slow (keep repeating); pony, pony, pony, pony; bear, bear, bear (repeat until all children are "frozen," then continue); snowflake, snowflake, snowflake; and so on.

THE JUMPING OVER LEGS GAME   (4–6 minutes) *locomotor and stationary*

Have all the children except one sit in a circle, their legs wide open and their knees straight. Make sure they stay this way, to avoid accidents (see figure 38). The child who is **it** chooses a number between 1 and 20, jumps over that many legs, and sits down. The last child who is jumped over becomes **it**. This child chooses a number and jumps over that many legs.

Say:

> Everyone **sit down** and **open your legs wide**, but **keep your knees straight**. *O* is for *over*: we are going to **jump over legs**. (choose a child to start) Now **choose a number** between 1 and 20. Now **jump over that number of legs**. The last person you jump over will change places with you.

Make sure each child has at least one turn. If necessary, suggest a number to the child who is **it**, in order to reach a child who may have been left out by chance.

O IS FOR *ORCHESTRA*   (3–3½ minutes) *locomotor and stationary*

Divide the class into 2 groups. Briefly discuss the various instruments in an orchestra, and then put on a record of orchestral music, preferably classical. Have half the children play make-believe instruments while the other half dances to the music. After a minute or so let them change roles.

Say:

> What different musical instruments do you know of? (violin, piano, harp, flute, trumpet, tympani, and so on) Now I'm going to divide you in half. This half (indicate) will **be my orchestra**; you can each play on any instrument you like. And you (indicate the other half) will **be dancers**, dancing to the music.

Let them wait until you put the record on; then have the dancers spread out and dance freely until you call for a change of roles.

The Half Circle and the Letter C **3**
(25–30 minutes)

Objective: To develop conceptual images of the half circle and the letter *C*
Special Equipment: March music

39.

THE HALF-CIRCLE GAME   (4–5 minutes) *locomotor*

Write the letter *C* on the chalkboard and discuss its shape. Then have the children make a circle, holding hands, with you standing in the center (see figure 39). The children should walk around you until you call stop. Then point arbitrarily, perhaps with your eyes closed, between any two children. Those two children should stop holding hands to open up the circle and make the letter *C*. Repeat this a number of times if you wish.

Say:

> **Make a circle around me, holding hands. Walk around me** until I call out stop. Then I am going to stretch my hand out without looking, and whoever my hand points to will **break the circle apart**. Then move backward a little bit to open the circle until it becomes the shape of the letter *C*. For example, if I pointed here, (indicate a spot between two children) you two would drop hands and open the circle up. Then we would close it up again and start once more. Ready? Everybody walk! Stop! And open here! Have we made a *C*? Walk again holding hands. Stop! And make a *C*.

C IS FOR *CLAPPING*   (3–5 minutes) *stationary*

Have the children standing in a circle, and let them clap their hands in various directions, which you call out to them. Later, have them do this sitting down.

Say:

> *C* is for *clapping*. Can you **clap high above your head**? Now clap **in front of your nose**. How would you clap **behind you**? Can you find

another way? Now try clapping **underneath you**. Now **all around** yourself. All **around your middle**. **Sit down** and clap **in front of your tummy**. Now **in front of your knees**. **Now under your knees**. Now **lie down** on your back and **kick your legs up**. Every time you kick a leg up, clap under it. Ready? Kick. And clap. And clap. (repeat 8 to 10 times) And rest.

HOP OUT A *C*   (2½ – 3 minutes) *locomotor*

Have the children walk about freely, stopping to hop out imaginary *C*s all over the room in their own timing.

Say:

> Make believe there are many *C*s written all over the floor. Some are big and some small, and they're all facing different directions. **Walk around and hop out as many of these *C*s as you like.**

PAINTING *C*s   (4 – 5 minutes) *stationary*

Have each child find a space and sit down. Ask them to paint large *C*s in different directions. Each time they end a letter they are to hold the position for a few seconds.

Say:

> Make believe you are in an attic and want to decorate the ceiling and wall and even the floor. **You have a huge heavy paint brush** that you have to **hold with both hands**; it pulls your body with it as you paint. With it you **paint huge half circles**, or letter *C*s, facing different directions. Some are lying flat, some are standing up, and some are going around you. Paint each one slowly and carefully, and every time you finish one, **freeze** for a while before going on to the next one. Sometimes you have to get up to **stir the paint** in your huge bucket with your heavy brush. Start by sitting or lying on your back to paint the ceiling.

After a while have the children stand up to draw even larger curves, incorporating their entire bodies. (Freezing in different positions requires a certain amount of control and provides a very good body workout.) Encourage the children to make their designs as large as possible, starting—and, especially, ending—far out to the sides, reaching behind or around themselves (see figure 40). Stirring, too, should be done with the entire body.

SHAPING A HALF CIRCLE   (4 – 5 minutes) *stationary*

Ask the children to shape half circles with their bodies in as many different ways as they can imagine (see figure 41). After they have experimented for a little while, ask them to go from one position to another when you call change (every 10 to 15 seconds). Call their attention to some of the more interesting ideas, which all can then try out for themselves.

Say:

> How would you **shape a half circle with your body**? Now try another way. Can you **find more ways** to do it? Now choose one position, making yourself into a half circle. When I call out change, go into another half-circle position. Remember you can sit, lie, kneel, or stand—use any position you like.

42.

C IS FOR *CIRCUS*   (5–6 minutes) *locomotor*

Describe and discuss the circus first, making sure that all the children know what one is. Then have them march around in a large circle, to parade music if possible. Call out various circus animals and performers for the children to act out as they march.

Say:

> *C* is for *circus.* Do you know what a circus is? How many of you have seen one? Make believe you are in a **circus parade,** all **marching along in a circle.** First comes **the band** playing drums, trumpets, and cymbals. Choose an instrument to play as you march along. Now be a group of **monkeys,** jumping and fooling around, bowing, and tumbling over. Then come the **dancing bears** stomping along, and **elephants** swinging their trunks. Then there are **acrobats** and **ballerinas** dancing on tiptoe and turning around. Now come the **clowns!** Now **pick your favorite character to be** as you are marching along.

43.

After a while, have the children sit in a large circle and take turns stepping into the circle to act out a circus character.

Say:

> **Sit down in a large circle** and each one in turn can **show us your ideas.** Make believe the **inside of the circle is the stage** and we are your audience watching you perform your favorite circus act. You could be a clown jumping up and down and making us laugh, or a ballerina, or an acrobat flying through the air, or an animal doing its tricks—whatever you want to be. Who would like to start?

End by having everyone get up at once and move freely for 30 seconds or so, acting out circus characters.

Note: For very young children, the idea of a circus may be too complex. You may want to use other, simpler words that begin with the letter *C:* for example, let them be angry **cats** with **curved** backs; have them **crawl** like **caterpillars;** or let them drive **cars** along a **crooked** road, bumping and screeching as they go along.

The Triangle and the Letter *A* 4
(25–35 minutes)

44.

Objective: To develop conceptual images of angles, triangles, and the letter *A*

Special Equipment: Masking tape or chalk

WALK! STOP! POINT YOUR TOES!   (3–4 minutes) *locomotor*

Have the children walk about freely, stopping to point their toes at your signals. After 4 or 5 stops ask them to find other ways to point their toes; then have them continue for a while. They should walk at a fairly brisk tempo and alternate their feet when pointing the toes (see figure 42).

Say:

> How would you point your toes? Good. Now **walk about** anywhere you like and when I call stop, **stop and point your toes.** Try to remember to

keep changing feet. Ready? Walk. Stop and point. And walk. Stop and point your toes. **How else** can you point your toes? Try pointing in different directions.

Have the children try standing, sitting, and lying down as they work out various ideas. After a while have them walk and stop as before, incorporating their new ideas (see figure 43). Next have them stand and point up with different parts of the body (see figure 44).

Say:

 How would you **point up to the ceiling with your toes**? Now let me see you point up with your **chin**. With you **elbow**. With your **seat**.

Let them try out various positions; then continue with the next activity.

SHAPE A TRIANGLE (4– 5 minutes) *stationary*

Draw a triangle on the chalkboard and ask the children to shape one with different parts of their bodies while they sit in a circle (see figure 45).

Say:

Make a circle and **sit down**. Do you know what a triangle looks like? (draw one) Do you see the sharp point pointing upward? How would you **make a triangle** with your **hands or fingers**? Now make a bigger one with your **arms**. How would you shape a triangle with your **legs**? Here is a good idea. (point out one child's version) Let's all try it. Who has another idea?

Have them try out one another's ideas to develop movement experience. Finally, ask them to make a triangle using their entire body, with their seat as the highest point and the floor as the base.

DRAW AN *A* (3½– 4 minutes) *stationary*

Let the children stand and write many large *A*'s in the air, facing various directions and at different heights. Each time they should accent the cross stroke.

Say:

Everyone up on your feet. Draw a really large *A* in front of you, making the point as high up as you can, and let me see a long wide cross stroke. I would like you to **make many *A*'s** in different places around yourself, but each time you **make a cross stroke slash it across** as if you had a sword in your hand and you were cutting your *A* in half. If you like, you can make a sound every time you cut a line across. (demonstrate a hissing or swishing sound) Really do it with force. Let your whole body be pulled along with it.

Encourage them to alternate hands as they draw the *A* and slash the line across.

YOU MAKE AN ANGLE AND I'LL DRAW THE LINE (4– 6 minutes) *stationary*

Have the children sit down and make sharp angles with different parts of their bodies. You walk around at random and draw a cross line to complete the letter *A* for all the children, one at a time, wherever they have their specific angle made (see figure 46).

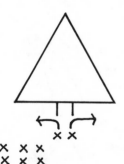

Say:

Sit down, and look at the letter *A* once again. Do you see the sharp top pointing upward? Two lines meeting at a point make an angle. *A* is for *angle.* I would like you to **make this kind of angle with different parts of your body, and I will draw the line across** wherever I see a pointed angle. You can use your hands, arms, legs, feet, knees, elbows—even your whole body if you like. Who has an idea so that I can draw the line across? Ah, here is an *A* (draw a crossline) and here is another one. (and so forth)

Immediately after you draw a crossline for a child, he or she should try to make a new angle. Have each child try out several ideas. Draw the children's attention to new ideas for using different body parts. Encourage them to change their positions to try out new ideas (standing, lying on their stomachs, sides, and so on). After a while, if you wish, let the *children* take turns walking around and drawing cross bars (one or a few at a time). End by letting them shape the letter all by themselves (see figure 47).

WALKING OUT A TRIANGLE   (7–9 minutes) *locomotor*

Using masking tape or chalk, mark out as large a triangle as possible on the floor. Have the children go along the outline using their own steps and accentuating the corners, first alone and then with a partner coming from the opposite side (see figure D).

Say:

Line up and one at a time, walk along the sides of this triangle. Walk it out in **any way you like.** You can slide, gallop, jump, skip, hop, and so on. But whenever you come to a corner, show it to me very clearly in some way. You might stamp, or clap, or jump, or turn around, or find your own way of **marking the corners.**

After they have all had one or two turns, let them take partners, decide which step to take, and then walk out a triangle from the middle of the base along opposite sides until they meet at the top.

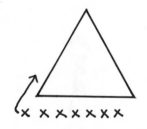

Say:

Take a partner and **decide** between you **what step** you will do around this triangle. You might both want to skip, or make a few steps and a jump, or slide sideways. Each couple starts at the center of the bottom line. **Walk in opposite directions** until you **meet at the top.**

End by having the children sit down along the base of the triangle and take turns acting out words containing an *A* sound. Help the children make a list of words to choose from; concentrate on only one *A* sound per session. Words easy to enact include: *far, car, farm, star, scarf, garden, dance, laugh, bath; cat, pat; gate, ate, pail, nail, hay, game.*

Say:

Sit down in one long line. Let's **think of words with an *A* sound inside,** like bat, for example. (list words) Now **one at a time, choose any word** you like with the sound of *A.* **Walk to the tip of the triangle,** and **act out the word.** For example, if you choose the word *bat,* you might make believe you are a bat flying out of a cave—or you might be a baseball player with a bat, getting ready for the pitch. Or you might choose the word *apple* and show us how you would pick apples—and so on. Who would like to start?

Objective: Reinforcing and learning letter shapes

Special Equipment: Masking tape or chalk; music for skipping (optional); flute
music for snake charmer (optional)

FORM A SNAKE   (2½–3 minutes) *locomotor*

Have the children hold hands to form one long line, with you or a child leading the
line in serpentines all over the room. If the leader faces the opposite way from
those in the line, the line will be more mobile. After a minute or so, stop and
change leaders; change again after that, but only one more time.

Say:

> Look at the letter *S*. (draw it on the chalkboard) *S* is for *snake.* Let's **make
> a snake by holding hands in one long line**. Line up here. (indicate)
> Who will be the leader? Come to the head of the line and hold hands
> facing the other way. When I say go, you **lead the whole line around
> like a great big snake**. Everyone hold on tight. Are you ready?

S IS FOR *SEAWEED, SPAGHETTI,* OR *SNAKE*   (6–7 minutes) *locomotor*

Have the children spread out and stand facing you. Then give them several words to
interpret that start with *S* and that suggest the round, curving quality of the letter.
Three very good possibilities are *seaweed, spaghetti,* and *snake.* Let the children
explore each of these words while you guide them with your voice.

Say:

> Spread out, find a spot, and stand comfortably. Do you know what *seaweed*
> is? It is a plant that grows in the sea. **Make believe you are seaweed**. You
> are attached to rocks at the bottom of the sea, but your leaves and stems
> are **moving softly** to the motion of the water. You feel it swaying you,
> rippling through your leaves. You welcome the fish as they swim through
> your branches, nodding to them as they go in and out. Suddenly a strong
> wave tosses you forward and backward, trying to pull you off. But you
> **hold firmly**, fighting the current. Then all is quiet again, and you **rock
> and sway** again gently, spreading your branches.

You might repeat this once again, perhaps designating half of the class as fish, who
move freely while the other half moves in place. Then continue with *spaghetti.*

Say:

> Now **make believe you are a stick of spaghetti** lying **stiff** inside your
> box. Now you are being lifted up over a pot, and for a moment you stay tall
> and straight while you are held in the air. **Then slowly** you sink into the
> water, and very slowly you feel yourself **grow soft** and softer, and you
> start to curl up as you **sink to the bottom**. Now you are being stirred and
> stirred and tossed about, until you lie all tangled up on a plate.

Repeat this once more; then let them try out various ways of sinking down slowly.
They might reach up with one arm while the other arm slowly pulls them down, or
they might sink down making *S*-shaped curves or spirals all the way down. After a
while, continue with the next study: *snake.*

Say:

Make believe you are a big fat snake lying all curled up in the sunshine. Now you hear something strange, and you **slowly raise your head and upper body** to look about you. You might hear the music of a snake charmer's flute and gently move to it, hissing now and then.

If you wish, have the children work in pairs, one being the snake, the other being the snake charmer playing on a make-believe flute. Accompany the movements with music, if possible.

WRITE AN *S*   (3 – 4 minutes) *stationary*

Have the children sit on the floor and draw *S*s in various ways.

Say:

Can you **draw a large letter *S*** whie you are sitting? Make it stand up in front of you. Now draw one along the floor around your legs. Who can draw the largest *S* around yourself? Now use your legs to draw a few *S*s in the air; try using first one leg, then both together.

SKIPPING SIDE BY SIDE   (2½ – 3 minutes) *locomotor*

For a fast change of pace, let the children take partners and skip freely together all over the room.

Say:

S is also for *skipping* and for *side by side*. **Take a partner and skip side by side all over the room.**

If you wish, play skipping music for this activity. After a while have the children sit and rest as you go on with the next activity.

WALK OUT *S* AND *J*   (10 – 12 minutes) *locomotor*

E.

Draw a large letter *S* on the floor with masking tape or chalk. Make it large enough for the children to walk along its outline comfortably. While you do this, have them think of words that start with *S*. Then have them line up to go along the *S*, one after the other, acting out the following words: *shore of a stream; shuffle; skate; stiff; sailing; stumbling; storm; scarecrow; snowflake; sea monster* (see figure E).

Say:

Line up in one long line here. (indicate) Now **make believe you are walking along the shore of a winding stream.**

F.

Continue through the words. Occasionally repeat some of the studies, according to your own discretion. Next, change the drawn *S* into a *J*, and continue with the next activity (see figure F).

Say:

J is for *jump!* One at a time, **run along this letter *J*** and then **jump off** at the end.

Repeat this 4 or 5 times.

J IS FOR *JELLYFISH*, S IS FOR *SEA* (2½–3 minutes) *locomotor and stationary*

End by letting all the children choose creatures or characters who live in the sea and, moving freely, act them out together.

Say:

Make believe the whole room is the ocean. Choose anything you would like to be as you move around. You might be seaweed once again, or a clam rocking in the waves and closing itself up, or an oozy jellyfish, or any fish at the bottom of the sea.

---

6 Round and Straight Combined: The Letter *D*
(25–30 minutes)

Objectives: Exploring round and straight designs; learning the letter *D*
Special Equipment: Masking tape or chalk; soft, flowing music

WALKING OUT DESIGNS   (5–6 minutes) *locomotor*

First have the children walk freely around the room, making up their own designs as they go. After a minute or so, have them line up on one side of the room. Then have them cross over, one at a time, in designs given by you. Draw the designs illustrated in figure G one at a time, on the chalkboard in the order given:

Say:

Walk all over the room, **making different designs** as you walk. You could make curves, round lines, straight lines with sharp angles zigzagging in and out, or loops. Make many different designs. Now **line up here**, (indicate) and then go one at a time, **walking out this design**. (draw the design on chalkboard) Use any step: skip, hop, run.

Draw the first design, and have the children walk (or skip, hop, or run) it out, one at a time. When they are done, have them wait at the other side. Repeat each design once or twice before going on to the next one. Give different challenges for each design.

Say:

Look at my **next design**. Again, walk it out in your own way, but make **sharp corners** as you go. Here is a **third design. Skip it out**, and **turn around** whenever you **make a corner**. Now here's the **last design**: take a few steps and then **jump from one line to the next**.

Let the children sit down and discuss the different qualities of the lines, particularly in the first two designs. Then, for another minute or so, let them again move about freely, making their own pathways, adding appropriate feeling and movement quality, first to the rounded line, then to the straight one.

Say:

Sit down, everyone, and **look at the designs** once again. How would you **describe the first one**? (snake-like, curved, rounded, wavy, and so on) Did you feel the same way when you were making the next design as you did making the first? What movements fit a rounded pathway? (soft, bending, turning, floating, swaying, like a scarf, like a butterfly, and so on) Now **get up** and spread out, and once again **make your own round**

G.

Fun with
Letter Shapes

designs, but **add a soft rounded feeling** and soft movements to it. Now **stop**, and **walk out straight lines with sharp** long straight **movements**.

48.

ROUND AND STRAIGHT COMBINED   (7–8 minutes) *stationary*

Have the children sit down and make alternately round and straight shapes, using part or all of the body (see figure 48). Since they have experienced these shapes separately, in previous lessons, they can now alternate the shapes without needing much preparation. They should hold each pose only for a few seconds. When calling the changes, use a softer, drawn-out tone for round shapes, and a fast, sharper call for straight shapes. It also helps to use a percussion instrument in a similar manner.

Say:

> Spread out and **sit down**. Do you remember how we made round shapes in different ways with different parts of our bodies? **Show me one round position**. Now try another one. Remember that you can also stand or lie down or be in other positions, if you like. **Now be straight** with any part of your body. Now go into a round shape. This time I am going to let you **change from being round to being straight, back and forth**. So every time you change, think of a new way to be either round or straight. Are you ready? Change! Now be round again. And be straight! And round! And straight! (and so on)

After a while, have the children work in pairs and change in opposition to each other. Since both shapes are being made simultaneously, you cannot use a different quality for your call, as you did before. So simply let the children get into starting positions, and call "change" every time. Give them time between calls to hold and observe the picture before going on (see figure 49).

Say:

> Now **take a partner** and spread out so that each couple has enough room to move. The children in each pair will be opposites: when one is round, the other will be straight. Do you understand? When I call out "change" you both go into the opposite position. Are you ready? Change! Change! (and so on)

This activity often produces interesting combinations that are well worth watching. After 5 or 6 changes, have the rest of the class watch while you call changes for one couple at a time. Remind the couple to also change levels and to relate to each other.

WALK OUT A *D*   (7–8 minutes) *locomotor*

Mark out a large capital *D* on the floor using masking tape or chalk. Then have the children walk it out in various ways, using different movement qualities for the straight and rounded lines (see figure H).

Say:

> Line up here (indicate) in one long line. **Walk this *D* out**, one after the other. Be very **stiff along the straight line**, and then continue **down the rounded line with soft, round movements**.

Let them repeat this once; then continue with *D* is for *duckling*.

Say:

> D is for *duckling*. **Make believe you are a little duckling** walking behind your mother duck. You **walk up the straight line** of this D, waddling all in a row, until you reach the rounded line. This is your pond. You walk along the edge to the middle of this line, then you **jump into the water and swim about**. Now you get out, shake yourself dry, and go back to line up with your other ducklings.

Repeat this once or twice, letting them "swim" about inside the D in their own ways. Then continue with D is for *dancing*.

Say:

> D is also for *dancing*. Make believe you are a **ballet dancer** and **walk up the straight line of the D pointing your toes** at every step. When you reach the rounded line **turn or dance** in any way you like, making round, soft movements all the way back to your line.

If you wish, repeat this one more time; then let all sit down and watch as one child at a time gets up to dance, making believe the D is the stage. Play a record—either a lyrical section of a ballet, or a soft waltz. End by letting all the children get up and dance freely together for a minute or so.

NOTE: The letter P can be walked out in a similar way. The imagery used can be P is for *park,* with the children being various characters walking up the straight line (their path) into the playground (the round area of the P). They could be mothers or fathers pushing baby carriages, balloon vendors, children with their toys playing games (hopscotch, skipping rope, and so on). A straight line can be added to form an R, and the children can *run* home to end.

BE A CLOUD   (3 – 3½ minutes) *locomotor*

Let the children make believe they are clouds, moving constantly and slowly changing their shapes from round to straight. If possible, play background music such as an adagio or a romance, or slow music from a ballet.

H.

Say:

> **Make believe you are a cloud** slowly sailing across the sky, **moving very gently**, and **constantly changing your shape**. First find yourself a starting shape. You can be standing, or moving on the floor, or you can change levels as you move. Listen a bit to this music. Now start to move very, very slowly, straightening out in one part and then becoming round again; very, very slowly changing your shape as you sail quietly across the wide blue sky.

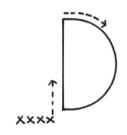

7 The Letters B and P
(25 – 35 minutes)

Objectives: To develop the concepts light and heavy: to study B and P; to explore more round/straight combinations

BE LIGHT! BE HEAVY!   (2 – 2½ minutes) *locomotor*

Let the children alternate between light and heavy steps, assisting them with imagery.

Say:

> What things do you know of that are very light? (feather, paper, and so on)
> Can you think of an animal that moves lightly? (chipmunk, squirrel, bird,
> butterfly, and so on) What moves heavily? (elephant, bear, monster, and so
> on) **Get up and move very, very lightly** around the room. You can make
> believe you are a fairy running lightly over the grass, jumping from flower
> to flower — or you might be a ballerina dancing lightly on tiptoes. Choose
> anything you like, moving lightly all over the room.

After a while let them move in a similar way, but this time heavily. Suggest that they
be elephants, bears, monsters, or giants as they move slowly and heavily about. After
a while ask them to alternate between moving lightly and heavily when you call
"change."

THE SOUNDS OF *P* AND *B:* A Variation of the Move and Freeze Game   (5–7 minutes) *locomotor*

After briefly discussing the difference between the sounds of *B* and *P,* ask the
children to walk on tiptoes when they hear *B* sounds, and to crouch down when
they hear the *P.* Pronounce only the sound of each letter, not the name. Repeat each
sound for 7 to 10 seconds (longer for the *B*s, shorter for the *P*s). You can vary the
sound level, phrasing, and accents from series to series.

Say:

> Can you hear the difference between *P* and *B*? Which is a lighter sound?
> How about this sound: /b/ /b/ /b/? Now listen to this: /p/ /p/. Get up.
> Now listen very carefully. **Tiptoe around very quietly**, and keep moving
> as long as I say the **light *B* sound**. When you hear me say the **heavy
> sound of *P*, crouch down** and wait. Are you ready? Listen.

Use sound series such as the following: /b/ /b/ /b/ /b/ /b/ /b/ /b/   /p/ /p/ /p/
/b/b/b/b/b/b/b/b/b/b/   /p/ /p/ /p/   /b/b/b/b/b/b/b/ (and so on)

   Next have the children sit down and think first of words that start with *B*, then of
words that start with *P.* Then have them get up and move freely while you call out
words that start with *B*, but freeze for words starting with *P.* Repeat each word
several times in a row, regardless of its initial letter.

Say:

> Move around any way you like, and keep moving as long as you hear me
> say words that start with *B.* When I say words that start with *P*, freeze and
> wait. Are you ready? Listen.

Examples: Bunny, Bunny, Bunny; (10 to 15 repeats) ball, ball, ball, ball, ball; peanuts,
peanuts, peanuts.

B IS FOR *BUBBLES, BLOW UP,* AND *BURST*   (4–5 minutes) *stationary*

Have the children sit or lie down and blow themselves up with different parts of
their body, making believe they are bubbles, then flopping down when they burst.
Lead them with your voice, accenting every burst with a strong percussive beat.

Say:

> Spread out and sit down anywhere in the room. Have you ever blown soap
> bubbles or chewed bubble gum? What does a bubble look like? Show me.
> Now **make believe you are being blown up into bubbles**. Some can
> be smaller and some bigger. Sometimes you could use your whole self and

sometimes only part of you—perhaps your side, or an arm, or your legs, or your back. I am blowing you up into a bubble. You are getting bigger, and bigger, **and then you burst!** Now make another bubble. It gets bigger and bigger, and then it bursts! You could **make believe you are bubble gum.** Start by being all squashed up. Then a bubble starts somewhere; it gets bigger and bigger, and then you burst with a smacking noise. (repeat a few times)

WRITE A *B* AND WRITE A *P*   (3–3½ minutes) *stationary*

Have the children first draw a letter *B* around themselves while they are sitting. Then have them get up and make a row of *B*s, rising up like bubbles (see figure 50).

Say:

> As you are sitting on the floor, make believe you are surrounded by bubbles, each one shaped like a *B*. **Draw as many *B*s as you can all** around yourself. Some can be near, some further away, some higher, and some lower.

Continue by having them draw a row of *B*s rising up and growing smaller and smaller as they rise. First the *B*s should go in a straight line, then into different directions; the children can make believe a strong wind is blowing the *B*s all over. Have the children reach and stretch as much as possible, guiding them with your voice as they draw their *B*s. End this activity by having them draw a few large *P*s facing different directions.

P IS FOR *PAINTBRUSH*   (2½–3 minutes) *locomotor*

For a fast change of pace, have the children run around freely, making believe they are paintbrushes painting designs all over the room.

Say:

> **Make believe you are a paintbrush** in an artist's hand, and the floor is the paper you are coloring. You run all over in soft swaying curves as you paint. Sometimes you go to stir the colors and turn around and around in the jar, and sometimes you dip yourself into water and make it splash about. Then you go on your way again, swishing, and swaying, and circling, as you **paint designs all around you.**

Let the children work on their own for a few minutes, making their own designs and finding their own spots for stirring the paint, and so on.

P IS FOR *PIZZA*   (5–6 minutes) *locomotor and stationary*

Ask the children to lie down and make believe they are pizza dough being kneaded, shaped, and stretched in different directions. Guide them with your voice as they move.

Say:

> Now everybody find a spot for yourself and lie down. *P* is for *pizza*. Make believe you are pizza dough lying in a lump on the table. A chef with a big white hat stands over you and starts to **knead you** and turn you around and knead you some more. Now the chef picks you up and **throws you down** with a smack! Then the chef **rolls you into a ball** and starts **stretching you**, first in one place, then in another, and yet another, pulling you here and pulling you there. Then the chef lifts you up and

turns you around and lets you hang over his hand, stretching you some more. Finally the chef puts you on a tray and into the oven. Now you are done and everyone takes a bite of you, and **you become smaller** and smaller until nothing is left but your crust.

Repeat this one more time, perhaps walking around and touching some of the children in various places to make them stretch specific body parts. After touching them, lift your hands as if you are actually pulling on them. Older children can work in pairs, one being the pizza dough, the other the chef.

P IS FOR *POPCORN*   (2–3 minutes) *locomotor and stationary*

End this lesson by having the children pretend to be popcorn, expanding, then popping, and bouncing around for a short while.

Say:

> *P* is also for *popcorn*. Make believe you are a small kernel of popcorn, **lying** at the bottom of the pan. First you are being **rolled around** a bit, then you settle down. Now it gets hotter and hotter, and you start to swell and **grow bigger** and rounder—and finally **you pop**! Then you hop, and pop, and bounce around, and make a funny noise every time you hop. Then you settle down again and **rest**, ready to be eaten and enjoyed.

You might want to repeat this, perhaps letting half the class at a time move while the others rest, then switching over.

Combining Letters
8
(30–35 minutes)

Objective: To reinforce letter shapes and sounds

WALKING OUT LETTERS   (5–7 minutes) *locomotor*

Call out one letter at a time and let the children walk it out in their own spaces. Start with 6 or 7 simple designs such as *I, O, B, L, M, N, U, S, J, D,* or *P.* Then introduce the letter *T,* which is more difficult to walk out because it requires retracing steps. Give a new challenge with each letter.

Say:

> Spread out and find a space for yourself. Walk out the letter *U,* in any size you like. Walk out an *M,* making very sharp corners. Walk out a *C,* walking backward. March out an *L,* making a sharp turn and ending clearly. Now make an *S,* ending in a round soft position. Walk out a *V* and end with your feet up, making a V with your legs. Now walk out a *T.*

Wait for a few seconds and observe the children; a number of them will be stumped at first. Single out one or two who have figured out what to do, and let them demonstrate their ideas to the class.

Ways to walk out *T:* Walk up the vertical line, then jump, spreading both feet apart, and stay in that position to indicate the top; walk as if on a tightrope, back and forth along the horizontal line, pretending to balance and then going down the middle; walk up the straight line, then lie down across the top.

YOU NAME THE LETTER AND I CALL THE BODY PART (5– 6 minutes)
stationary

Let the children sit in a circle and one at a time pick a letter from the alphabet. Call out a body part for all to write the letter with. You can add additional challenges, as well, such as a specific direction or size.

Say:

Make a circle and **sit down**. I am going to let each of you **choose a letter** from the alphabet, and then **I will tell you how to write it** in the air around you. Who wants to choose our first letter? (for example, *O*) Stand up and write it with your hips.

Try to vary their positions as much as possible.

Challenges to suggest: using hips or tummy while standing (especially for letters like *U, O, B, S, Z,* or *M*); using elbows, sitting and drawing the letter on the floor to one side; using heads to write tall letters from the floor up; using noses.

GUESS THE LETTER (5– 7 minutes) *stationary*

Let the children work in pairs and take turns writing letters with a body part. Each partner is to guess the other's letter.

Say:

Take a partner and decide who is 1 and who is 2. Stand side by side. Now all ones, **think of a letter**. Then **choose any part of your body to write it with. Your partner has to guess** the letter you are writing. Name your body part first so your partner will know where to look. Then switch.

Let the children work on their own, but walk around among them to watch and perhaps guess here and there, as well. If the children stand side by side, oriented in the same direction, it will be easier for the partner who is reading the letter.

T IS FOR *TIGHTROPE* AND *TUMBLING DOWN* (3– 3½ minutes)
locomotor

Let the children spread out and make believe they are walking along a tightrope, tumbling down at your signal.

Say:

Spread out and find a place for yourself. *T* is for *tightrope*. Do you know what a tightrope is? (explain) **Make believe you are walking on a tightrope**, but not very high up in the air. When you hear my signal (demonstrate) you **tumble down**! Are you ready? Walk very carefully, putting one foot in front of the other. And tumble down! Get up and try that again: walk carefully. (repeat 4 or 5 times)

Z IS FOR *ZOO* (7– 9 minutes) *locomotor and stationary*

Let the children make believe they are animals in a zoo. Start them out with a few ideas; then let them take turns choosing an animal to act out on their own.

Say:

Have you ever been to the **zoo**? What animals have you seen there? **Make believe you are an elephant** living in the zoo. You walk slowly about and pick up peanuts with your trunk. Sometimes you splash yourself with water, lifting up your trunk and blowing the water all over you. Now make believe you are a **great big bear**. You walk heavily, looking right and left. Sometimes you stand and sway from side to side. Then you roll over onto your back and sun yourself.

Other zoo animals: a **monkey**, jumping around, hopping up and down, swinging and jumping, scratching itself all over; a **seal**, sitting on a rock, sunning itself, lifting its head and torso occasionally to bark; a **giraffe**, with very stiff legs and a very long neck, nibbling the leaves off the treetops, drinking from a brook by opening its long legs wide and bending forward to reach the water; a **snake**, moving about slowly, stretching out in the sun, curling up, and hissing; a **kangaroo**, jumping and hopping about, its little baby tucked tightly in its pouch; a **panther**, pacing up and down, with smooth soft steps, kneeling down to stretch itself (see figure 51); a **penguin**, waddling about, standing very stiff as if frozen, then waddling some more. If the children have further ideas continue for a while. End by letting each child in turn choose an animal to act out alone.

51.

More Letter Combinations
(25–30 minutes)

 9

Objectives: To reinforce letter shapes and sounds; to work with partners
Special Equipment: Masking tape or chalk

G IS FOR *GALLOP*   (3–3½ minutes) *locomotor*

Write a capital *C* on the chalkboard, saying it stands for *coach*. Then change it into a capital *G* and explain that the short line is the seat of the driver whose horses like to *gallop*. Then let the children gallop freely about the room. On your signals they should stop and sit (or crouch) down and then "gee-up" their horses.

52.

Say:

> *C* stands for *coach*. Now watch closely as I change this *C* into a *G*. This (indicate short crossline on *G*) is the seat of the driver whose horses love to gallop. **Gallop around**, and on my signal, **stop and sit**, or crouch down, **and gee-up your horses** again. Ready? Gallop. And stop. And gallop! (5 to 7 repeats)

53.

Y IS FOR *YOGA*   (6–7 minutes) *stationary*

Write the letter *Y* on the chalkboard. Have the children sit in a circle and do a few simple yoga postures. Let those who can, demonstrate a lotus posture. (that is, sit cross-legged with the feet pulled up on the thighs)

54.

Say:

> *Y* is for *yoga*. Do any of you know a yoga posture? Sit with your legs crossed, pulling your knees down as much as possible for the **lotus** posture (see figure 52). Can you touch your head to the floor with your legs crossed? Now touch your ear to the opposite knee. Now try a **cobra** (see figure 53). You lie on your stomach with your hands next to your shoulders, then you raise yourself slowly up, curling your head back. This is the cobra. While you are on your stomach, try to hold on to your ankles to pull your legs up. This is called the **bow** (see figure 54). Can you rock

while you do this, like a boat? Now lie on your back and lift your legs up, stretching them out behind your head. Touch your toes to the floor behind you. This is called the **plough** (see figure 55). Help yourself by pushing your hips up with your hands. Now bend your knees so that they touch your ears; then hold on to your hips and slowly raise your legs up into the air. This is the **shoulder stand** (see figure 56).

Walk around assisting the children and helping them raise their legs up. Help them keep their elbows close to their sides for better support.

WRITE YOUR INITIAL   (3–3½ minutes) *stationary*

Have the children write various letters with their legs, first lying down and writing them in the air, then standing up and writing on the floor.

Say:

Lie down and **write a large R** in the air **with one leg**. Now do it with the other leg. Write **your first initial** with one of your legs. Now write **a friend's initial**, but make it large so that I can read it. Now **get up** and make believe you are on the beach and **write your name** with your toes in the sand. Use your other foot to write **your friend's name**.

THE LETTER Q: RUN AND FALL FLAT   (2–2½ minutes) *locomotor*

Write the letter Q on the chalkboard. Then let the children run in one large circle, and on your signal, fall down. Use a strong percussive beat for each fall.

Say:

Make a large circle. Now look at the letter *Q:* it is a circle with a little straight line across. When I say go, **run around** in your circle, and on my signal (indicate) **fall down** to make the line of the *Q,* stretching out on the floor. Are you ready? Run. And fall down. And on your feet and run! (repeat 3 to 5 times)

4
THE MOVE-ALONG ALPHABET

This section deals with one letter of the alphabet at a time, and includes letter shapes, letter sounds, and word associations. (Only lessons 24 and 25 are exceptions.) These lessons can be given in any order.

For best results, write the letter for each lesson on the chalkboard at the beginning of the session. Also write out any words that are used, to help prereaders with word recognition and older children with associations.

1 The Letter *A*
(22 – 27 minutes)

Objective: To provide letter review and vocabulary development

Special Equipment: Music for running

A IS FOR *ARM*   (3 – 3½ minutes) *locomotor*

First have the children demonstrate an airplane's pathway with their hands. Then let them move freely, preferably to music, following their arms.

Say:

> How do you think an airplane might do tricks? Show me with your hand how it would fly. Try that once more with the other hand, letting it go higher, lower, and all around you. *A* is for *arm.* **Move about, letting your arm lead you**, zooming high and low, curving in, out, and around as you go.

Play fast running music. After a while ask the children to change arms.

57.

REACH WITH YOUR ARM   (4–5 minutes) *stationary*

Have the children stand in a circle. First ask them to explore various arm movements; then develop reaching with the arm so that the children are incorporating the entire body in their movement.

Say:

> What can you do with your arms? Let's take one suggestion at a time. **How far forward can you reach with one arm?** Can you reach farther **with the other one**? Can you reach over to a neighbor without moving your feet? Sit down and see if you can reach over to one of your neighbors while you are sitting. How far forward can you reach now?

Ask the children to try reaching with their legs closed, then with their legs open. Then have them lie back with their legs straight up and ask them to reach up to their toes. Finally, ask them to kneel and reach around themselves. Go on to the word *acrobat.*

Say:

> *A* is also for *acrobat.* **What kind of tricks can acrobats do with their arms and legs?**

Let the children explore this concept on their own for a while. Encourage them to share ideas.

Acrobat tricks: kicking the legs while standing; going into "splits" (spreading the legs apart); jumping jacks; jumping high from a low crouching position; touching the head with the toes while sitting, standing, or lying on the stomach; upside-down leg movements while in shoulder stand; clapping in different places while swinging the arms and body; standing and touching the floor with one hand as the other reaches up to ceiling; and so on (see figure 57). Older children may be able to do cartwheels and backbends.

BE AN *A*   (4–5 minutes) *stationary*

(This activity is a more advanced version of one that appears on page 47.) Have the children work in pairs, one partner shaping an *A* and the other drawing the lines. After a minute or so, call for a change of roles.

58.

A IS FOR *AIRPLANE*   (3–3½ minutes) *locomotor*

Have the children pretend to be airplanes, "flying" freely, landing, and taking off at your signals.

Say:

> *A* is for *airplane.* Make believe you are an **airplane** cruising around. When you hear my signal, (demonstrate) land softly any way you want to. You can land flat on your tummy, or balance yourself on one leg, or you could land on all fours and then stretch a leg out behind you to look like a plane (see figure 58). Are you ready? Fly around. Land softly. And take off again. (and so on)

A IS FOR *ALARM CLOCK*   (5–6 minutes) *stationary*

Have the children spread out and stand facing you. First ask them to make believe they are clocks, ticking in various ways; then ask them to be alarm clocks.

Say:

Have you ever listened to a clock ticking? Pretend you are a clock and tick. How could you **use your body to tick**?

Ways to show ticking: crisscrossing the hands or entire arms in and out; swinging the arms forward and backward; swaying the body from side to side; crisscrossing the legs in and out (sitting or lying down); turning the face; moving the head, the shoulders, and so on. Let the children experiment with all these ideas; then continue with the alarm clock.

Say:

A is for *alarm clock*. **Make believe you are an alarm clock, ticking away** any way you like. At my signal, make your alarm go off! You may want to buzz or ring, but **show your alarm**, too. You can jump up and down, run around, or roll back and kick your legs. Find your own way to be an alarm and wake the whole house up. Are you ready? Tick. And sound your alarm! (repeat 4 or 5 times)

You may want to vary this activity by having half the class "tick" while the other half sleeps until the alarms go off. Then switch over.

A IS FOR *APPLES*   (3–3½ minutes) *locomotor and stationary*

Have the children stand in a circle and pretend to be apples hanging on a tree. Then go into the center and pretend to shake the tree so that the apples fall off.

Say:

A is for *apples*. Can you shape yourself like an apple? Now **make believe you are hanging on a tree**, perhaps swaying a bit on your branch. Now I'm going to shake you off! **Fall down and roll about** in the grass. (repeat the activity a few more times)

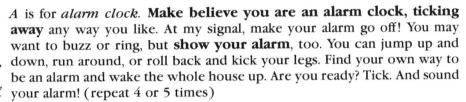

2 The Letter *B*
(25–30 minutes)

Objective: To provide letter review and vocabulary development

B IS FOR *BUNNY, BEE,* AND OTHER *BEASTIES*   (3½–4 minutes) *locomotor*

Let the children move about freely, making believe they are various animals whose names start with the letter *B*. Signal them to change by suggesting a different animal every 30 seconds or so.

Say:

B is for *bunny*. **Make believe you are a bunny**, hopping and bouncing around, sometimes stopping to dig up a root to nibble on, then hopping on again. *B* is also for *bee*. **Make believe you are a bee**, buzzing around in a B-shaped pathway, making a B-line to a flower, then flying around it, drinking the nectar and swaying on the petals. Then you buzz off again. *B* is for *beetle*. **Make believe you are a little black beetle** crawling along through the grass, sniffing the flowers, search for food. *B* is for *bird*. Can you **hop and flutter like a bird** in a birdbath? *B* is also for *beaver*. **Be a busy beaver**. Gnaw at trees with your long sharp teeth to build yourself a dam in the water, and pull your sticks and branches into the lake to build your house.

B IS FOR *BENDING*   (5–6 minutes) *stationary*

Have the children bend various parts of their bodies, first sitting in a circle, then changing to other positions.

Say:

> B is for *bending*. **What parts of your body will bend?** Who can think of a part? Let me see.

Have them bend fingers, arms, and necks. Have them bend the whole body. Have them try sitting, lying, kneeling, standing, and bending in different directions—forward, backward, sideways, across (see figure 59). After a while, ask them to find ways to bend their legs (see figure 60).

B IS FOR *BRIDGE*   (5–7 minutes) *stationary*

Have the children work alone for a minute or so, pretending to be bridges. Then have each one team up with a partner to make bridges together (see figure 61).

Say:

> B is for *bridge*. Let me see you **make a bridge**. Now make a different one; now make another one. Now **take a partner** and **make a few bridges together**. You can use your arms, your legs, your heads, even your whole bodies if you like. Try out a few ideas; then choose your favorite one to show us all.

Have them take turns showing their bridges; then count out the couples into ones and twos. Have one group be bridges for the others to crawl under.

Say:

> I am going to give each couple a number: this couple is a 1, this couple is a 2, this couple is a 1. (and so on) Now **all number ones**, **make a bridge**—whichever bridge you like best—and **all twos** spread out and **crawl under** these bridges. But be careful to go through without touching any bridge.

Not touching is a safety measure to prevent roughhousing. After a while, let them change roles.

B IS FOR *BALL*   (3–4 minutes) *locomotor*

Ask the children to spread out and pretend to be balls. Let them bounce freely for about 10 seconds or so; then ask them to follow your directions.

Say:

> Leave your partners and spread out and **pretend you are a ball bouncing around**. Now everybody **stop**. Make believe you are **a ball lying quietly on the floor**. Now a little draft of air is making you **rock softly** and then **roll over**—and over again, into another position. Now someone picks you up and **bounces you higher** and higher, and then walks away and leaves you. You **bounce lower** and lower, and finally you **stop** and **slowly roll about**, and then **lie quietly** once more.

B IS FOR *BOAT*   (3–3½ minutes) *locomotor and stationary*

Ask the children to be boats. First let them experiment on their own; then guide them as they move.

Say:

 B is for *boat*. How would you use your body to **be a boat**? Can you find still another way?

Let them try out several ideas, such as sitting with legs bent or straight, or lying on the stomach and rocking from side to side or forward and back (see figure 62). After a while ask each one to choose a position, and continue.

Say:

Now choose your favorite way to be a boat and **slowly sail across the lake**. There is a blue sky, and a gentle breeze pushes you forward. Now the wind grows stronger and the waves get higher and higher. You **begin to rock**; you are **tossed** about; you **turn and spin** around. Then suddenly you **flip over**.

B IS FOR *BALLOON*   (2½–3 minutes) *locomotor*

Ask the children to get up and move about freely, pretending to be balloons.

Say:

B is also for *balloon*. **Make believe you are a balloon and I am blowing you up**. You get bigger and lighter, and now you **float** and **gently bounce** around the room. Make big soft leaps, landing very softly every time. Now you land on a pin, and **you burst and shrivel up** with a funny noise.

Repeat this once or twice, particularly the part about shriveling up with a funny sound.

3 **The Letter *C***
(25–30 minutes)

Objective: To provide letter review and vocabulary development

C IS FOR *CAR* AND *CURVE*   (2–3 minutes) *locomotor*

Have the children move about freely, pretending to drive cars on curved roads, stopping with a jerk.

Say:

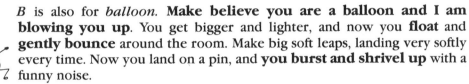 *C* is for *car* and for *curve*. **Make believe you are driving your car on a curvy road**. Every now and then you **stop with a jerk**.

DRAW A LETTER *C*   (3–4 minutes) *stationary*

Have the children stand in a circle and write large *C*s in front of them; then have them sit or lie down to write *C*s with their legs.

Say:

Write a huge letter *C* in front of you. Make it larger than you are. Can you **write another one with both hands** locked together? Now get down on the floor and find a way to write the largest *C* you can, **using your legs**. Write a few *C*s with each leg, and in different positions—lying, or sitting, or even using both legs together.

65
The Move-Along
Alphabet

After a while ask the children to use their legs to write a few short words such as *cool, cozy, cat,* and so on. End by having them sit up and write a short word around themselves, using one hand.

Say:

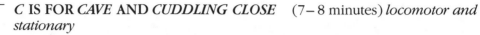 Sit up, or kneel if you like, and **write the letters** *C, A, B* **around you.** *C-A-B* spells *cab.* You can imagine you are riding in a cab.

63.

C IS FOR *CAVE* AND *CUDDLING CLOSE* (7–8 minutes) *locomotor and stationary*

Ask the children to try to shape caves with their bodies, first individually, then with partners.

Say:

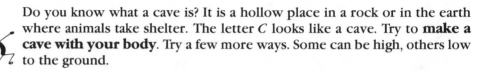 Do you know what a cave is? It is a hollow place in a rock or in the earth where animals take shelter. The letter *C* looks like a cave. Try to **make a cave with your body.** Try a few more ways. Some can be high, others low to the ground.

The children can try kneeling, crouching, and lying curled up on the side, as well as curling over from a standing position (see figure 63). After trying out a number of ideas, ask them to team up with partners, one making a cave and the other cuddling close.

Say:

 Take a partner and decide who is 1 and who is 2. Now all ones, make a cave any way you want to. When the caves are ready, all twos make believe it is raining hard and take shelter in your partner's cave, cuddling close to stay dry. Now change over: all twos make a cave and ones take shelter.

 Repeat this activity a number of times, letting the children shape different kinds of caves each time. Encourage them to try out each other's ideas. After a while divide the class in half. Every other couple will be wanderers looking for shelter; those remaining will make caves together, as before.

Say:

 All these couples (point to every other couple) **make caves. The rest of you,** wait until the caves are ready, and then leave your partners and **wander around** from cave to cave by yourself, **taking shelter** wherever you like, cuddling close for a bit, then going on to find another cave.

 After a while have the groups change roles. Encourage them to make the caves as varied as possible: high-domed, low, leaning, deep, shallow, and so on.

C IS FOR *CLOWN* (1½–2 minutes) *locomotor*

For a fast change of pace, let the children move freely, pretending to be clowns.

Say:

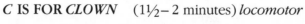 *C* is for *clown.* **Leave your partner and make believe you are a clown,** jumping around in any way you like; make funny faces and funny movements to make everyone laugh.

C IS FOR *COPYCAT*   (6–7 minutes) *stationary*

Ask the children to make a circle and be copycats, first copying your movements as you call them out, then working with partners.

Say:

> Make a circle and stand comfortably. *C* is also for *copycat*. **I am going to give you a movement**, and **you be the copycats**. Are you ready? I am shaking my head. I am shaking a leg. I am rocking from side to side. I am jumping up. I am sitting down. I am making a circle with my head. (and so on)

After a while, have the children work in pairs. Ask them to sit opposite each other and to take turns being the copycat. Have them do a series of movements before you signal them to reverse roles by calling "change."

C IS FOR *CLAY*   (3–4 minutes) *stationary*

Have the children make believe they are lumps of clay, which you shape and knead, guiding them with your voice as they move.

Say:

> Leave your partners, and spread out. *C* is for *clay*. **Make believe you are a lump of clay** lying on my table. Now I take you and start to **knead you**, punching you here and there to make you soft. I **roll** you about a bit, and now I start to **shape you**. First I make **an arm**, then **a head**, then your **other arm**, and I put **a smile** on your face You freeze, so I can have a good look at you. Then I **squash you up** and start all over. I knead you some more; then I slowly give you a shape, letting you grow here, and there, making you as **tall** as I can. Now you are starting to dry out and you **become stiff.** I sprinkle water all over you and **squash you up into a lump** again.

Repeat a few more times, putting them into a different shape each time before you squash them up again.

---

4 The Letter *D*
(20–25 minutes)

Objective: To provide letter review and vocabulary development
Special Equipment: Ballet music

D IS FOR *DEER*   (2½–3 minutes) *locomotor*

Ask the children to move about freely, pretending to be deer.

Say:

> *D* is for *deer*. **Make believe you are a deer**, alone in the deep forest. You leap very softly and quietly, jumping over fallen logs and little streams. Sometimes you stop to drink or to nibble leaves or moss, and then you leap on again.

D IS FOR *DIRECTIONS*   (4–5 minutes) *stationary*

As the children stand in a circle, have them all write the letter *D* as you call out various directions in which to write it.

Say:

 *D* is for *directions*. I am going to call out a direction, and you write the letter *D* there. **Use a different part of your body each time**.

Directions: above; below; in front; beside you; next to your nose, left ear, right foot (and other body parts).

D IS FOR *DANCING*   (4–5 minutes) *locomotor*

First show the children these ballet poses: pointing the toes; first position (heels together, toes turned out) plié (kneebend); lifting a leg in front or behind, keeping the back straight (see figure 64). Then play ballet music and let them dance freely; every now and then call for them to pause in one of the dance positions. Suggest that they hold their arms out for balance.

Say:

 *D* is for *dancing*. Can you point your toes like a ballet dancer? This is the first position. (demonstrate) You can have your arms up or out, but keep your shoulders down all the time. Now try a plié; try to keep your back nice and straight. Can you lift one leg up behind you? Keep your back pulled up to hold your balance. You can also lift one knee up in front and point your toe. When the music plays, **dance any way you like**, and on my signal, **stop for a moment in a dancer's pose**.

D IS FOR *DREAM*   (6–7 minutes) *locomotor and stationary*

Have the children sit in a circle and one at a time go around the outside, making believe they are in a dream world. Suggest a few ideas to them first, such as a thick forest, snow-covered fields, and so on.

Say:

 *D* is for *dream*. Did you ever dream you were in a strange place? Make a circle and sit down. **One at a time, walk around outside the circle, making believe you are in your dream.** You could be walking in a thick forest; or you might be in a meadow chasing butterflies; or there might be snow for you to stomp through and make into snowballs; or you might be in a big city wandering into different stores; or you might even dream you are on a strange planet where you meet strange beings and have to walk in a strange way. Pick your own dream place to be in as you walk around.

Ask all the children to describe the dream world they are in as they start out, to make watching more fun.

D IS FOR *DROPPING DOWN*   (3–3½ minutes) *locomotor*

Have the children pretend to be various objects dropping down.

Say:

 Everyone, up on your feet. *D* is also for *dropping down*. Make believe you are a stone and drop down!

64.

Other objects: a *piece of paper* falling slowly, fluttering and turning over as it falls; a *snowflake* or an *autumn leaf* falling, whirling and being blown around, then softly settling down on the ground; and finally a *wet sponge* that drops on the floor with a smack. (Repeat these items a few times in random order.)

5 The Letter *E*
(20–25 minutes)

Objective: To provide letter review and vocabulary development
Special Equipment: Brisk 4/4 music that suggests an engine (optional); chalk or masking tape

E IS FOR *ENGINE*   (3–3½ minutes) *locomotor*

Briefly discuss engines: you might mention that engines are what make machines such as cars and trains go, and that engines are made up of many moving parts. Then let the children move freely, preferably to music, making believe they are engines. Use any brisk music with a clear 4/4 beat.

Say:

Have you ever watched the engine of a car working? Some parts go up and down, and others clank together or turn around. They all work at once to make the car go. Many machines have engines that puff and push, jerking and rolling along with their own special noise. **Make believe you are an engine**; push and jerk and move every part of you in many different ways.

E IS FOR *EXERCISE*   (5–6 minutes) *stationary*

Have the children sit in a circle and take turns suggesting exercises for the entire class to do.

Say:

E is for *exercise*. Who can **think of an exercise** for all of us to do? Can you show me?

Take one child's suggestion and let the class do it; then take another child's suggestion. If necessary, offer your own ideas, such as: sit-ups; leg-raises; bending over to touch the floor; jumping jacks; and so on.

E IS FOR *EGG*   (4–5 minutes) *stationary*

Have the children make believe they are eggs being scrambled.

Say:

E is for *egg*. **Make believe you are an egg** lying on the kitchen table. Now the cook pushes you and you **roll over**. Then she picks you up, and you rise up high. Then you **crack in the middle** and you pour out into a frying pan. There **you lie, flat** and limp. First you are **stirred** and stirred around. And now you are being **scrambled** and tossed about from side to side. Now you are being **turned over** and stirred some more. Now you are all done and you are **rolled up** into an omelet that smells good. (repeat one more time)

WALKING OUT AN *E* (6–7 minutes) *locomotor*

Make a large *E* on the floor, using masking tape or chalk. Make the cross bars about 2 feet apart so that the children can jump from one to another. Then have the children line up and, one after the other, run up the straight line, turn the corner, and jump down from rung to rung.

Say:

Line up in one long line. *E* is for *escalator.* I am going to make a big letter *E* for you. You can **make believe it is an escalator** and **run all the way up** the straight-line side and then **jump down the stairs** on the other side by jumping from one cross line to the other. Of course, everyone knows you must never do this on a real escalator.

After a while you can change the activity to climbing the stairs (perhaps on all fours), and then running "down" the straight line. Another possibility is to start with one *E* and then add new *E*s on top of it to make the staircase longer.

E IS FOR *ELEVATOR* (3–3½ minutes) *stationary*

Have the children make believe they are elevators, slowly rising and sinking down with occasional stops along the way.

Say:

Now find your own space in the room and **make believe you are an elevator** in a tall building. You go slowly up and down all day long, making stops along the way to let people in and out. Sometimes you stop for a long time, opening your doors wide, waiting for people to come. You close up carefully behind the people and continue on your way. When you get tired, you creak as you go along, and you sometimes stop with a jerk.

The Letter *F* 6
(20–25 minutes)

Objective: To provide letter review and vocabulary development

Special Equipment: Music for skipping

F IS FOR *FLOATING* (3–3½ minutes) *locomotor*

Have the children spread out and make believe they are floating, either in outer space or under water. Start by having them move in slow motion, first in place, then through space.

Say:

We are going to work with words that start with the letter *F.* Spread out and stand facing me. *F* is for *floating.* Make believe you are **an astronaut moving in outer space.** Or you could be **a diver moving in very deep water.** When you wave your arms, they move very, very slowly. You may want to reach one way, but your body drifts to the other side. You may want to rise, but you feel your body twist and sink down. Everything seems to be floating—your arms, your legs, your whole body—as you move in very slow motion around and about.

You may want to demonstrate first and have the children imitate you. Stand with legs apart and slowly grope in various directions, twisting, swaying, letting your legs bend or rise; use your whole body. After a minute of moving in place, have the children slowly progress freely through the room.

F IS FOR *FROG* (1½– 2 minutes) *locomotor*

For a fast change of pace, have the children pretend to be frogs and jump around freely.

Say:

 F is for *frog*. **Frogs like to jump all around. Can you show me how frogs jump?**

F IS FOR *FACTORY* (6– 7 minutes) *locomotor and stationary*

Have the children line up in one long row, side by side, if possible with their backs to a wall. Then ask them to make believe you are visiting different factories and they are the items manufactured. They pop out of a machine when you press a button. Announce a different kind of factory each time so they will know what to turn into. Then walk along their line and as you point to each child, he or she should step forward and assume the appropriate shape. Repeat this process for each new factory "item."

Say:

Line up in one long line, side by side (along the wall, if possible). *F* is for *factory*. **Make believe we are in a factory and you are being manufactured**, or made, by a machine. **You are inside the machine, and when I press a button, you pop out.** Every time, I will tell you what the factory makes so you will know what you are going to be. Get ready; stand still in one long line, and wait until I pass by you to press a button. I am coming into an ice-cream factory, where *ice-cream cones* are made. One by one you pop out as ice-cream cones, all curled up on top. Now I leave you, and you melt and get back into your line. Now I am visiting a factory that makes *tables*. When I press the button, you pop out in the shape of a table. Get back into line; this time I'm in a factory that makes *bathtubs*. Now I want to buy a house for Snoopy at the *dog-house* factory. Now I need a fluffy *pillow*.

You might give each one a little poke to see if they are "fluffy." End by going into a factory that makes **windup toys**. Let the children think for a moment what kind of toy each wants to be. Then repeat the button-pushing procedure and have them pop out in their various shapes. You may want to wind them up to let them move freely for a minute or two.

Other items for future sessions: clocks; lamps; tops; fans (which you can switch on briefly); T-shirts; candles; coat hooks or coat hangers; suitcases (which you can open to inspect); carpets or rugs (which come out flat, and which you can then roll up); little figurines for your dressing table (animals, dancers, sports figurines); and so on.

F IS FOR *FAMILY* (7– 8 minutes) *locomotor*

Have the children work in groups of three or four to make up animal-family scenes. Give them several suggestions first; then let them make their own ideas. When all are ready, call them into a circle and let each group perform their scene.

Say:

 F is for *family*. Let's form groups of three (or four). Each group should choose an animal to be; then make up a little **family scene**. You could be a family of squeaky little **mice**, or a family of **birds**, or bouncy **rabbits** digging a burrow, or a family of fuzzy **bears**, or **elephants**, or **puppies**. Decide what family you would like to be, and when you are ready we can watch each group's scene and guess what each family is.

F IS FOR *FUNNY*   (2½– 3 minutes) *locomotor*

End the session by having the children skip freely to music. Every now and then stop the music to signal the children to strike a funny pose.

Say:

 F is also for *funny*. Skip around the room to the music and when the music stops, **freeze in a funny position**.

The Letter *G* 7
(22– 27 minutes)

Objective: To provide letter review and vocabulary development

G IS FOR *GALLOP*   (2½– 3 minutes) *locomotor*

Have the children pretend to be horses galloping in a field. Tell them to stop at your signals and then to "gee-up" again. (See page 58.)

G IS FOR *GROWING*   (5– 6 minutes) *stationary*

Have the children make believe they are small seedlings, little by little growing into plants of their own choice. (See page 12.)

WRITE A WORD   (5– 7 minutes) *stationary*

Write short words starting with *G* on the chalkboard, one word at a time. First have the children write each word in the air. Then have them sit down and take turns writing one letter each, in sequence, thus spelling the word. Ask them to write with whatever part of their body they choose.

Say:

G is for *good*. (for example) **Write** the word *good* **in the air** in front of you or on the floor around you. Now sit down. Let's see how many ways we can write the word *good* writing just **1 letter each**. Take turns getting up and writing a letter with *any body part* you wish. (select a child to start) Get up, step into the circle, and write the letter *G* in your own special way; you could write it on the floor with your nose, or you could lie down and write it in the air with one leg. Then, next in line, write the *O* in your own way. Each person, try to think of a new way to write your letter when your turn comes. When we get to the end of the word, the next child just starts it again by writing the letter *G*.

Repeat the word until everyone has had a turn; then continue with another word. Give each child a number of turns so each one can try out different ideas.

Other *G* words: gold; gift; game; gas; gate.

G IS FOR *GARDENS*   (6–7 minutes) *locomotor and stationary*

After discussing and acting out different ways to take care of gardens, divide the room into three areas, using furniture or other objects as boundary markers. Have the children choose an area to work in until you call "change." The areas could be lawn, apple orchard, and pond.

Say:

> *G* is for *garden.* What do people have in their gardens? How could you take care of your gardens? What else do people do in their gardens? Show me.

Have the children act out digging, planting, sowing, watering, mowing the lawn, raking leaves, and so on. Then continue, dividing the room.

Say:

> Make believe this area (indicate) is a *lawn.* What could you do here? (mow it, rake the leaves, play on it, roll on it, dig out the weeds) This area (indicate) is an *apple orchard.* What would you do here? (shake the trees, jump up to pick the apples, eat apples, gather the fallen apples and cart them away in a wheelbarrow) This part of our garden (indicate) is the *pond.* What could you do here? (catch frogs, wade, dangle your feet, fish, skip stones) Choose one of these areas to work and play in, and when I call "change," go to a different area.

G IS FOR *GHOST, GIANT,* AND *GAME*   (3–3½ minutes) *locomotor and stationary*

End this session by having the children all move together freely, first as ghosts, then as giants, and finally on a playground, choosing their own games.

Say:

> *G* is for *ghost.* Show me how a ghost looks, haunting the countryside. Now be *giants,* another *G* word. Walk around with giant steps, stepping over rooftops and stomping around. *G* is also for *game.* Make believe you are on a playground, playing whatever game you like best.

---

8 The Letter *H*
(22–27 minutes)

Objective: Vocabulary development

H IS FOR *HORSE*   (5–6 minutes) *locomotor*

First have the children gallop freely for about a minute or so; then have them pretend to be different kinds of horses.

Say:

> *H* is for *horse.* Who can **gallop like a horse**? Stop. What else can horses do? **Make believe you are a horse pulling a wagon**, trotting down the

street. Now go uphill, puffing and blowing, and shaking off the flies. Now be a **circus horse** doing tricks. You could rise up on your hind legs and turn around, or walk sideways, or do a special step, and then bow and tap the floor with your dainty hoofs. Now be a **race horse**, waiting at the starting gate for the signal to go, speeding around the course, jumping over fences, racing to the finish line.

H IS FOR *HOUSE* (7–8 minutes) *stationary*

Have the children shape houses, first individually, then with their partners (see figure 65).

Say:

> *H* is for *house*. Can you **shape a house with your body**? Now **get a partner and make a house** together.

Let the children work by themselves for a while; then ask each couple to show their house to the rest of the class. Have them repeat the activity once or twice, making different houses each time. You may want to have them try this activity in groups of 3, 4, or more.

H IS FOR *HOUSE* AND FOR *HURRY* (8–10 minutes) *locomotor and stationary*

Have the children sit in a circle and list many things people do in houses. Concentrate on one room at a time. Then let them act out their ideas, first at normal speed, then in a hurry.

Say:

> List a few things people do in the kitchen. Now get up and **make believe you are working in the kitchen.** Bake a cake, or set the table, or scrub the floor and wash the dishes. *H* is also for *hurry*. Now do all the same things in a great hurry!

Continue this way with other rooms: the **bedroom** (dress and undress, make faces in the mirror, comb hair, go to sleep and wake up, put the toys away); the **living room** (dust, vacuum, read a book, watch T.V., call a friend on the telephone, serve snacks to guests, and so on). End by having the children take turns choosing a specific area and acting out activities that go on there while the others guess the room.

H IS FOR *HALLOWEEN* (2½–3½ minutes) *locomotor*

Ask the children to pretend to be Halloween characters and let them move about freely, in unison, each according to his or her own ideas.

Say:

> Everyone up on your feet. *H* is also for *Halloween*. Think of a special Halloween character you would like to be and then move about in your own special way. You might be a *pumpkin* bouncing along with rolling eyes, or a *witch* riding on a broomstick, or perhaps a *ghost* or *goblin* knocking at doors or windows for trick-or-treats. **Choose your own favorite, and move about!**

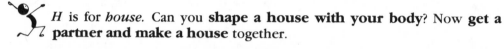

Objective: To provide letter review and vocabulary development
Special Equipment: A piece of white streamer 3 to 5 feet long; music for skipping

WALK OUT LETER *i* AND SPIN FOR THE DOT   (3–3½ minutes) *locomotor*

Let the children walk out letter *i*'s at random, spinning around to make the dot.

Say:

 Walk out the letter *i* wherever you like, and when you come to the end, spin around to make the dot. Then make some more *i*'s.

I* IS FOR *INSIDE   (3–3½ minutes) *stationary*

Have the children sit in a circle and make believe they are in a dangerous place, but that they have a magic wand they can use to draw a protective "cage" around themselves. Encourage them to make the cage very large, stretching and twisting as they do so.

Say:

Come and sit down in a circle. Do you know any stories about fairies and dragons? **Make believe you are in fairyland,** but on a dangerous spot. But **you have a magic wand** in your hand, and with it you draw a protective net of magic all around yourself. Draw carefully, going over your head from one side to the other, in many directions, back and forth. Make yourself really safe inside.

When the children have done this, go on to the next activity.

I* IS FOR *I AM   (6–7 minutes) *locomotor and stationary*

Continue with the image of fairyland; let the children choose characters or fantastic beings they can portray. Have them get up one at a time, announce the character by saying, "I am . . . ," and then step into the circle to act it out.

Say:

I is for *I am.* First think, "I am in fairyland." Now, **think of something or someone from fairyland that you would like to be**. When you are ready, you can take turns showing your ideas. One at a time, get up and tell us what you are, saying, "*I am.* . . ." Then act it out inside the circle. You might be a fairy, or a monster, or a dragon, or a dwarf, a little elf, or perhaps a blue bird, a unicorn, or some other animal you like. Who would like to start?

After the first child has had a turn, have them continue in consecutive order around the circle.

I* IS FOR *ISLAND   (6–7 minutes) *locomotor*

Have the children make believe they are landing on different enchanted islands. Start by having them make a circle and lie down. You stand in the center of the circle, holding a white streamer, 4 to 6 feet long, in one hand. Call them to "wake them up," and have them follow imaginary silver ropes to an enchanted place. Every time this happens, have the children "fly about" more or less freely, while you wave your streamer; then have them land.

Say:

 I is for *island.* Let me take you to an enchanted island. **Make believe you are asleep and dreaming.** Now, wake up, and you see **a shiny silver rope** dangling right in front of you. You reach up to it and it **pulls you up** and out of the window, and it carries you fast and far away. Then **you land** softly. You are **on an enchanted island**.

Island habitats:

1. Filled with flowers to pick, dance around in, and put into hair.
2. Very watery, with ponds, puddles to jump over, brooks to wade in, waterfalls, rain, dense fog.
3. Covered with snow and ice for sliding, stomping around, and so on;
4. Forested, with trees that bear ice-cream cones and cookies, a different kind on each tree.

In future sessions, islands can be lands of various creatures, which the children turn into when they land: giants; dwarves; fairies; giant beetles that hum, buzz, plomp down, and roll over; or cartoon characters. Islands could also vary according to different kinds of motion that are possible on each: slow motion; backward motion; jumping and hopping; fast motion.

I IS FOR *INVITING*   (6–7 minutes) *locomotor and stationary*

Have the children stand in a circle. Have one child start by skipping around the circle to music. The child then goes inside the circle to invite another child to take his or her place.

Say:

 I is for *inviting.* Make a large circle. Then, **one at a time**, **skip** around the **outside** of the circle. After a while, **go inside to invite whomever you like to** take your place. Who would like to start?

You can add challenges to this activity by asking children to make certain moves while inviting; for example, pointing their toes, one foot at a time; turning around; curtsying.

The Letter *J* 10
(25–30 minutes)

Objective: To provide letter review and vocabulary development

J IS FOR *JOGGING* AND *JERKING*   (2–2½ minutes) *locomotor*

Let the children jog around in their own pathways. At your signal, they should stop with a jerk. Signal them to stop every 10 to 15 seconds, using a percussive beat.

Say:

 J is for *jogging* and for *jerking.* When I say go, **jog around**—but listen for my signal. (demonstrate) Every time you hear this signal, **stop with a jerk**. Are you ready? Jog. And stop! And jog. (and so on)

WRITING WORDS WITH *J*   (4–5 minutes) *stationary*

Choose a few simple words that start with the letter *J*. Write them, one at a time, on the chalkboard. Ask the children to write each word in the air, changing positions according to your instructions.

Say:

Make a circle and **sit down**. I am going to write a word on the chalkboard and then I will tell you where I want you to **write in the air**. Here is the word *jog*. (for example) Write it in large letters **in front of you**. Now lie on your back and write it **above you**. Get up and write it **underneath you**. Lie on your side and write it on the floor **along side of you**. Try that lying **on the other side**, using the other hand. Kneel and write **behind you**. Stretch out on your stomach and write it way up **in front** of you.

J IS FOR *JACK-IN-THE-BOX*   (4–5 minutes) *stationary*

Have the children make a circle and crouch down low, pretending they are jack-in-the-boxes. Stand inside the circle and call on one child at a time to jump up, do 4 jumping jacks, and sit down again.

Say:

J is for *jack-in-the-box* and for *jumping jacks*. Make believe you are a little jack-in-the-box. Whenever I push your button, you **jump out** of your box and **do 4 jumping jacks**. Then you jump back in again. Are you ready?

Point to one child at a time in random order, and say, "I push your button."

J IS FOR *JUICE*   (2–2½ minutes) *stationary*

For a rest and change of pace, let the children pretend to be citrus fruit you are squeezing.

Say:

J is for *juice*. **Make believe you are a nice juicy orange, and I am squeezing you.** Now be a big fat **grapefruit**. And I am squeezing you. Now, you are a **lemon**, and I **roll** you about a bit to make you softer, then I squeeze you all out.

J IS FOR *JUMP!*   (5–6 minutes) *locomotor*

Have the children line up at one end of the room and then jump over 2 lines, which you have drawn about ¾ of the way toward the other side. Make the lines wider after every jump. Stand facing the children, 4 or 5 yards beyond the furthest line to catch them after they land, if necessary. Use a strong percussive beat to signal every jump and to emphasize the takeoff.

Say:

Line up, one behind the other, here. (indicate) I am going to draw **a river for you to jump over**. One at a time, run and jump over it. Wait for my signal! Are you ready? Run. And jump! (and so on)

JACK AND JILL   (6–8 minutes) *locomotor and stationary*

Have each child take a partner and then line up, as before, to act out the story of Jack and Jill.

Say:

> Take a partner and line up once again. *J* is for *Jack and Jill.* Each couple, act the story out together. Walk up to the river, making believe you are carrying your big pail; then fill the pail up with water and carry it back down the hill. On the way back you stumble and fall and roll. Let's watch the first Jack and Jill.

You might suggest that children change the ending, for example, by coming back and falling down in one heap, or by rolling over and kicking their legs up in the air, or by sitting down and making a funny face.

The Letter *K* 11
(20–25 minutes)

Objective: To provide letter review and vocabulary development

66.

K IS FOR *KANGAROO*   (2–2½ minutes) *locomotor*

Have the children hop about freely, pretending to be kangaroos.

Say:

> *K* is for *kangaroo.* **Make believe you are a kangaroo,** hopping about with your little baby safely in your pouch.

K IS FOR *KICKING*   (6–7 minutes) *locomotor and stationary*

Have the children stand in a circle. Ask them to suggest various ways of kicking. Have the group try one suggestion at a time.

Say:

> *K* is for *kicking.* How many different ways can you kick your legs? Show me.

Ways to kick: with the legs straight as well as bent; standing and kicking forward, sideways, across, backward; sitting, or lying on the back, clapping under each leg, or "bicycling"; lying on the side and kicking one leg straight up; kneeling and kicking a leg back; and so on (see figure 66).

After 3 to 4 minutes, have the children line up and cross the room one after the other, taking 2 or 3 steps and then kicking a leg forward. End by having them go back across the room, this time doing a "scissor jump" every few steps. A scissor jump is done by kicking both legs forward, one immediately after the other, legs straight.

K IS FOR *KITCHEN*   (9–10 minutes) *locomotor and stationary*

First have the children sit in a circle and list as many kitchen activities as they can think of. Concentrate on food preparation, such as making toast, breaking eggs, baking pizza, mixing and frosting a cake, and so on. Then act out some of these ideas, letting the children be the food, while you be the chef, verbalizing your actions.

Say:

> Make a circle and sit down. *K* is for *kitchen.* Let's think about the different things we can do in the kitchen. (discuss ideas) Now **I am going to cook in the kitchen and you are going to be my groceries.** First I need **5 eggs**. (choose 5 children) Go into the circle and be my eggs. Now I am going to crack you open and **I am scrambling you**, and turning you around, and now I mix you together into one heap. You can go back. Now I am going to cook **spaghetti**. I need 7 children who are **stiff strands of spaghetti**. (choose them and wait till they stand stiff and straight) Now I boil you, and **slowly you become soft** and curly and sink down into one tangled-up **heap**.

More cooking tasks:

Baking a cake: a number of children can be flour and eggs, each moving separately as you mix them all together, but keeping in some contact with one or more other children by turning around each other, linking arms, climbing over each other, and so on. Then have a few others be lumps of chocolate, which you melt, letting them run all through and around the flour and eggs. Then shape them into a cake and finally have several children put their arms straight up to be candles.

Hamburgers with mashed potatoes: have 3 to 5 children be a lump of meat, which you chop apart. Then have salt and pepper hop in between them, and remold them into "patties" (groups of 2 or 3 children). Mash potatoes in a similar way, adding "ingredients."

K IS FOR *KALEIDOSCOPE*   (5–6 minutes) *locomotor and stationary*

If the children are unfamiliar with kaleidoscopes, bring one in to show them. Then have the children make a large circle, holding hands. Pick a group of children to go inside this circle. Become part of the outside circle and walk around with those children, all holding hands. At intervals, call "stop." When the outer circle stops, the children inside should make different shapes.

Say:

> **Make a circle** and hold hands. *K* is for *kaleidoscope.* (pick a number of children) You go inside the circle and be the colorful pieces. We are going to be the outside of the kaleidoscope. We walk around, turning. Those inside the circle can move gently about as we walk. When we stop, each colored piece freezes in any shape it likes. Some of you might stand, and some might sit or lie down or kneel to be at different heights. Freeze so that we can look at the picture you are making. Then we will go around again, and when we stop, make another shape and freeze so we can look at the picture.

After 3 or 4 shapes, choose another inner group and repeat the activity.

12 The Letter *L*
(25–30 minutes)

Objective: To provide letter review and vocabulary development

MOVE LIGHTLY   (3–4 minutes) *locomotor*

Suggest various things that move lightly, and have the children act them out, moving freely.

Say:

Make believe you are something very light. You could be a **kite** flying high in the sky, or a **feather** fluttering around, or perhaps an **elf** running lightly through the forest, or **a ray of sunlight** dancing on a lake. Think of something really light to be, and show me how it moves.

L IS FOR *LEGS* AND FOR *LEADER*   (6–7 minutes) *stationary*

Let the children first stand, then sit, in a circle to play Follow the Leader with leg movements.

Say:

L is for *legs*. Stand in a circle and **show me different things you can do with your legs**. Now sit down, and one at a time **be the leader**, doing something with your legs for everyone else to copy.

Encourage the children to change their positions for a greater variety of movements; have them try leaning back on their elbows; lying on their backs or sides; lying on their stomachs, facing into the circle.

L IS FOR *LINE*   (6–7 minutes) *locomotor*

Continue the previous activity, this time walking across the room, following a leader.

Say:

L is also for *line*. Let's follow the leader again, moving across the room. Line up on this end of the room, (indicate) and **one after the other lead the others across** in the steps you want to use.

If the group is small enough, repeat the activity.

L IS FOR *LOVE*   (8–10 minutes) *locomotor and stationary*

Have the children sit in a circle and discuss their associations to the word *love*. Then stage a few scenes to have them act out their ideas.

Say:

L is for *love*. **Let's think of different ways to show love.** Can one of you think of an example?

Children may suggest sharing toys with a friend; making a special gift, then wrapping and presenting it; caring for a pet or for plants; helping parents with their chores; being kind to someone sad or old; and so on. After discussing several ideas, stage a few scenes, delegating the parts.

Say:

Now let's act out some of our ideas. Let's say we have a family of birds. Birds show lots of love in caring for each other. Let's start with **2 birds building their nest**. (select 2 children) Fly in and out of the circle to collect twigs and branches to make your nest really comfortable. Now one of you is the mother sitting on the nest, and the other is the father, who brings you food. Now the father takes a turn, and mother brings the food. One of you is always keeping the eggs nice and warm. **Now who will be the baby birds**? (select 4 or 5 children) Go into the center of the circle and make believe you are just coming out of your eggs while mother and father bird watch. You knock and peck and finally crack the shell. You step carefully outside and look around. Then you open your mouths wide and call for your parents. Quickly they bring you worms and little bugs and other goodies to eat.

End by having the children work in groups of 3 or 4 to make up their own scenes for *love.*

13 The Letter *M*
(25–30 minutes)

Objectives: To provide letter review, vocabulary development, and experience working with partners

M IS FOR *MAGIC* (4–5 minutes) *locomotor*

Call out one magic spell after the other, letting the children move freely and pretend to be the creatures you name. Use a percussion instrument to signal stop before each new spell.

Say:

 M is for *magic.* **I am going to cast a magic spell and turn you into different things.** Are you ready? I turn you into a tiny **mouse**, running, looking for cheese, nibbling on it. And freeze. (signal) Now I turn you into a **monster**. And freeze. (signal) Now you are all **monkeys**.

Other spells: musicians, playing in a parade; mail carriers, carrying heavy bags of mail, delivering letters; mocking birds, hopping and chirping; moths, turning and turning round a light and finally falling down.

M IS FOR *MOVING* (5–6 minutes) *stationary*

While the children are on the floor, have them show how they can move in lying, sitting, and standing positions.

Say:

 M is for *moving.* How can you move while you are lying on the ground? While you are sitting down? While you are standing up?

Possible movements: waving arms and legs; rolling onto the back, side, and so on; in a sitting position, reaching with the arms, twisting at the waist, and so on; in a standing position, moving in place—first moderately, then in slow motion, and finally very fast (running in place, twisting, shaking arms and head, swinging arms, jumping, hopping, and so on).

M IS FOR *MIRROR* (5–6 minutes) *stationary*

Have the children take partners. Each is to copy the partner's moves as if one were looking into a mirror and the other were the reflection.

Say:

M is for *mirror.* **Take a partner** and make believe that one of you is looking in the mirror, and the other is the reflection. **Whatever you do,**

the reflection in the mirror copies. Decide who will be looking into the mirror and who will be the reflection. Move slowly so that the one copying can follow you.

As the children move, suggest various ideas, such as moving backward and forward, bending, stretching, and so on. After a while, have the partners change roles. Later, you may want to have the children change partners and repeat the activity.

M IS FOR *MEETING*   (7–8 minutes) *locomotor and stationary*

Have the children stay with their partners and make up special ways of meeting.

Say:

> *M* is for *meeting*. **Stay with your partners and make up a special way of meeting.** You might be **2 children** skipping along and suddenly you meet. Make up a special way to greet each other, such as leaning back and rubbing your tummies together, or opening your arms and then shaking hands in a special way (see figure 67). Or you might be 2 **animals**—such as 2 **mice** scampering around and rolling over when you meet; or 2 **puppies** walking around each other and then standing and wagging your tails; or 2 **bunnies** hopping and then rubbing your noses together; or 2 **bears** bumping into each other in a friendly way (see figure 68). With your partner make something up. When you are ready come and sit in a circle.

Have everyone sit in a large circle. One couple at a time should get up, move in opposite directions around the circle, and then show the class their meeting. If they are animals, they should announce what they are to make it easier for the others to understand their movements.

M IS FOR *MERRY-GO-ROUND*   (3–4 minutes) *locomotor*

Divide the class in half, and have one half make a circle while the other half goes inside and sits or lies on the floor. Those outside are to be the horses, moving around in a circle; those inside are the machine that makes the horses move.

Say:

> *M* is for *merry-go-round*. Let's divide the class in half. This half, (indicate) make a large circle. The other group, sit down inside it. We (outside) are the **horses**, galloping, or trotting, or running around and around, going up and down as we move. You (inside) are the motor that makes us go. You are parts of the **machine**, punching, kicking, puffing, bicycling and so on; each of you helps make us go in your own way.

After a short while (20 to 30 seconds or so), have the groups change roles.

The Letter *N* 14
(27–33 minutes)

Objective: To provide letter review and vocabulary development

N IS FOR *NEEDLE*   (2–2½ minutes) *locomotor*

Have the children pretend they are needles, running back and forth, sewing something up.

Say:

N is for *needle*. **Make believe you are a needle**, running back and forth as you sew a patch on someone's knee or sew up a hole in someone's sock. Sometimes you have to push hard to get through a thick part, and sometimes you fly swiftly in and out.

N IS FOR *NOSE* (4–5 minutes) *stationary*

Have the children sit in a circle and try to think of ways to hide their noses. First have them try out different ideas in unison; then have each child take a turn demonstrating one idea.

Say:

N is for *nose*. What can you do with your nose? (wiggle it, sniff with it, point with it) Now try to **hide your nose in some way**. Can you find another way? How many ways can you think of?

Ways to hide your nose: cover with the hands; bury in the crook of the elbow; put between the knees; cover with one or both feet (various positions).

WALKING OUT AN N (6–7 minutes) *locomotor*

Ask the children to spread out. Have each one walk out an *N* in his or her own space, each time using a step suggested by a different child.

Say:

N is for noise.

Spread out and **make believe there is a large N written on the floor** near you. **Walk it out.** Now let's do it again—but in a new step. Who can suggest a new step for all of us to do?

After a while, encourage the children to try different ways of accentuating corners.

N IS FOR *NOISE* (7–8 minutes) *locomotor and stationary*

Have the children sit in a circle and make a variety of noises. Ask them to take turns demonstrating their ideas.

Say:

N is for *noise*. Can you **make a small noise**? Now make **a big one**. How could you make a **funny** noise? Now make a **scary** one. Now make up **your own special noise combination**. You can use your hands to knock or clap, or use your feet to stamp or tap, as well as using your voice. Make up a short phrase that you can repeat many times.

When everyone is ready, proceed as before, listening to each child in turn. Then have each child go into the circle to repeat his or her noise combination for all to move to.

Say:

One at a time, come into the circle and **repeat your sound-phrase a few times**. Everyone else, get up and make up some movements that you think fit this special noise. Who would like to start?

N IS FOR *NIGHT* (7–9 minutes) *locomotor and stationary*

First discuss the night and things that happen at night that don't happen in daylight. Then have the children work in pairs to make up nighttime scenes.

Say:

N is for *night*. What do you think of when I say "night"? Now **take a partner** and **make up a short scene about the night** together. One of you might be a **parent**, and the other, a **baby** being tucked into bed; or you might be an **owl** waking up and hooting in a tree. You might be two **cats** on a fence miaowing and making round backs. One of you could be the **moon** rising and slowly traveling across the sky; the other one might be a **cloud** sailing across or a **star** twinkling. Make up your scene together, and then we will watch each couple.

After watching each couple, have everyone move freely for a minute or so, being anything they like pertaining to the night.

The Letter *O* 15
(25–30 minutes)

Objective: To provide letter review and vocabulary development

O IS FOR *OBSTACLES*   (4–5 minutes) *locomotor*

While the children walk about freely, have them get past make-believe obstacles in accordance with your calls.

Say:

O is for *obstacles*. An obstacle is something that gets in your way. **Make believe you are walking in the country.** Your path goes **over big rocks** and you have to lift your feet up high to step over these obstacles. Sometimes you bump your toes. You come to a huge **mud** puddle, so you jump from one side of the path to the other until you pass this obstacle. You come to a **wall**, and you have to climb over it. Then you come to a **fence**. You crawl under this obstacle. Now you are in a peaceful meadow, and you lie down to **rest**. Suddenly a huge cow comes towards you. You **jump up** and quickly jump right **over the fence** and **run** all the way **home**.

WRITING THE LETTER *O*   (5–6 minutes) *locomotor and stationary*

Have the children draw the letter *O* around themselves, first while they are standing, then while they are moving.

Say:

Write the letter as large as you can in front of you. How large can you make it around yourself? Try writing it in different places. See if you can make it even larger by using your legs.

Let the children try as many ways as they can think of, standing and lying down. After a while let them move about as they draw the letter, making believe they are holding paintbrushes in their hands and decorating the whole room with *O*s— walls, ceiling, and floor.

O IS FOR *OPEN*   (7–8 minutes) *locomotor and stationary*

Let the children take partners and think of things that open. Have each couple act out their ideas for the others to try to guess.

Say:

O is for *open*. **Take a partner and together think of something that opens.** Then **act it out** together. When you are ready we will try to guess what you are.

Walk around while the children are thinking, and suggest ideas if necessary.

Things that open: doors; windows; gift boxes; lunch boxes; elevators; the jaws of a crocodile; treasure chests; letters; books; and so on.

O IS FOR *OAK TREE*   (4–5 minutes) *stationary*

Have the children pretend they are tiny acorns, slowly growing into sturdy oak trees as you guide them with your voice.

Say:

O is for *oak tree*. Do you know the old saying "From the tiny acorn a mighty oak tree grows"? **Make believe you are a tiny acorn** lying snugly in the ground. Slowly you start to **grow**, and bit by bit you become **taller and wider**, until you stand as proudly and firmly as a full-grown **oak tree**. You **watch the birds** fly in and out of your branches, and you **let the wind ripple** through your leaves and sway your twigs. Suddenly there is a **storm** coming up and it grows stronger and stronger. You feel the **rain battering against you** and **you bend and sway** in the wind. **Your twigs are bent and your leaves are drooping.** Then the storm blows away, the **sun** comes out and **dries you off**, and **your leaves sparkle** and twinkle in the breeze. You are **a mighty oak**, as big and strong as ever.

O IS FOR *OCEAN*   (5–6 minutes) *locomotor and stationary*

Talk about the ocean with the children. Show them pictures of sea life, if you can, and discuss aspects of the ocean itself. Have the children interpret these ideas; call out one thing at a time.

Say:

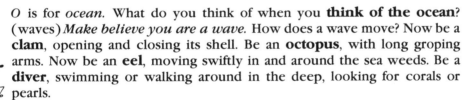

O is for *ocean*. What do you think of when you **think of the ocean**? (waves) *Make believe you are a wave.* How does a wave move? Now be a **clam**, opening and closing its shell. Be an **octopus**, with long groping arms. Now be an **eel**, moving swiftly in and around the sea weeds. Be a **diver**, swimming or walking around in the deep, looking for corals or pearls.

End by asking each child to choose one oceanic thing to be, and have them all move together for a minute or so.

16 The Letter *P*
(25–30 minutes)

Objective: To provide letter review and vocabulary development
Special Equipment: Ball or balloon

P IS FOR *PICTURE*   (3–3½ minutes) *locomotor*

Have the children move about freely, stopping at your signals and freezing so that you can mime taking their picture.

Say:

 P is for *picture*. **Run around** anywhere you like, and when you hear my signal, **stop** and **pose for a picture**. Ready? Run. And stop—and let me take your picture. And run. (and so on)

Repeat the sequence 7 to 9 times.

P IS FOR *PICKING* AND *PICKING UP* (5–7 minutes) *locomotor and stationary*

Start by having the children sit down and pretend to pick berries. Encourage them to twist and reach as much as possible. Then continue by having them pick other items.

Say:

 Sit down wherever you are. *P* is for *picking berries*. **Make believe you are sitting in the middle of a raspberry patch**, and you don't want to stand up because of the many thorns. But there are berries hanging all around and above you. Pick as many as you can, and eat them up. You can reach way up and behind you to get them all.

You may want to have the children count as they pick, reaching in a different direction on every count. After a while ask them to carefully creep out of the berries and to pick up other things: a heavy **stone** to carry and then to drop; a **frog** that keeps jumping away; a **ball** to bounce and throw up into the air; a handful of **spaghetti** to eat up.

PASSING A BALL (5–7 minutes) *stationary*

Have the children sit in a circle and pass a ball around, first one way, then the other. Finally they should get up and pass it overhead, backwards.

Say:

 P is for *passing*. Sit down in a circle and **pass this ball to your neighbor on your right**. Now pass it **the other way** around. **Line up, standing** one behind the other, and **pass the ball overhead** all the way to the back of the line.

Ask the children to bend backward and reach up as they pass the ball. When the ball reaches the end of the line, have the children turn around to repeat the procedure. Then ask them to pass the ball back through their legs. Lastly combine the movements, one child passing it overhead, the next passing it between the legs.

P IS FOR *PILLOW, PUDDING,* AND *PRETZEL* (6–7 minutes) *locomotor and stationary*

Have the children act out objects that start with *P,* while you guide them with your voice, moving about among them.

Say:

P is for *pillow*. **Make believe you are a round and puffy pillow.** Now I turn you over and **fluff** you up a bit, and **tickle** you here and there. *P* is also for *pudding*. **Make believe you are chocolate pudding.** You are **soft** and **shaky** and sway around in your dish. Then you giggle and laugh, and that makes you **shake** even more. Now I'm going to make you into a

pretzel. First I **roll** you into a long thin roll, rolling you **back and forth** so that you get **longer and thinner**. Then I **fold** you over and over, until you are all **twisted** into a pretzel.

Repeat *pretzel* a few times to let them twist in different ways. You may want to repeat *pizza* and *popcorn* from pages 55-56.

P IS FOR *PUPPY*   (5–6 minutes) *locomotor and stationary*

End by having the children be puppies, preferably running on two legs for better mobility.

Say:

P is for *puppy*. **Make believe you are a puppy.** You **bounce** around in the garden, **wagging** your tail; then you **roll** over and **kick** your legs up for joy. You **sniff** around and find a bone and **chew** on it. After a while you bury it in a hiding place. You hear your owner whistling, and you **run** to him and **run around** and through his legs. Then you hear a cat miaowing and you run to **chase** it, **barking** up a tree. Then you **trot** back to your owner and **cuddle** down to sleep.

---

17 The Letter *Q*
(25–30 minutes)

Objectives: To provide a letter review, vocabulary development, and practice in auditory discrimination

Q IS FOR *QUICKLY* AND *QUIETLY*   (5–6 minutes) *locomotor*

As the children stand facing you, call out various moves for them to do either "quickly" or "quietly."

Say:

This is a game called Quickly and Quietly—two good *Q*-words. I'm going to call out movements for you to do. Listen carefully so you don't make mistakes. **Quickly jump** into the air. **Quietly sit** down. **Quickly get up. Quietly** make a **step to your right. Quickly make a circle** and **quietly sit down.**

Other movements: raising and dropping an arm; raising a knee and putting it back down; sitting down and rolling over; getting up to run and touch a wall, then coming back to place; walking around in a circle; crawling; tiptoeing; walking backward; taking giant steps.

Q AND *U* ARE TWINS (a variation of the Move and Freeze Game)   (5–7 minutes) *locomotor and stationary*

On the chalkboard, make a list of words that contain *qu,* and point out to the children that these two letters always go together. Then let the children take partners and listen carefully as you call out the words on the list. Without warning, slip in words that do **not** contain *qu*. Repeat each word many times. The children should stay sitting down as long as the word you are repeating contains no *qu*s. But when you call words that contain *qu,* they should get up an dance or move together.

Say:

Now **take a partner** and sit down. Do you see that *q* is always followed by a *u*? They always go together—like twins. **Listen** very carefully now as I call out different words. **When I call a word from our list** with the letters *qu* in it, **all partners get up and dance** around any way you like. You can skip or turn together, or move in some way. Make believe you are twins who are always together: one of you is *q* and the other one is *u*. But listen carefully. If I call out **a word that *doesn't* contain *q* and *u*,** you have to **sit down quietly and** wait. Are you ready? Listen!

Repeat *Q*-words 15 to 20 times; repeat words without *Q* 7 to 9 times.

Q IS FOR *QUARREL*   (5–7 minutes) *locomotor and stationary*

Ask the children to keep their partners, and to decide which is *q* and which is *u*. In this activity, the children mime a quarrel between the "twins," *q* and *u*. They alternate making movements of their own choice. Call out letters, changing every few seconds.

Say:

Q is also for *quarrel*. Stay with your partners and decide who is *q* and who is *u*. We're going to pretend that *q* and *u* are quarreling. I would like you to **act out a make-believe quarrel** without words; just make angry movements and be careful not to touch each other. What kinds of movements show anger? You might stamp your feet, shake your head, jump up and down, put your hands on your hips. One of you might turn away or kick the ground; the other one might be very angry and punch into the air. Make up your own movements as you go along. Are you ready? Take your turn when I call your letter. *Q*s start. Now *U*s. (and so on)

After a while, have everyone sit down and take turns "quarreling," one or two couples at a time, while the others watch.

Q IS FOR *QUEEN*   (6–7 minutes) *locomotor*

Talk briefly with the children about queens, what they do and how they behave. Then have the children walk around, pretending to be queens and courtiers. They should walk slowly and sedately, standing erect, pointing their toes at each step. Next let them act out the queen's court, and finally interpret a fairytale.

Say:

Do you know what a **queen** looks like? How does a queen **walk**? How do **other people** behave toward her?

I.

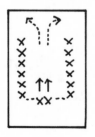

You may want to have the children take partners, one being the king and the other the queen, and form two lines. Then one couple at a time should walk down the aisle while the rest of the class bows or curtsies (see figure I). When all the couples have been down the aisle, continue with fairytale queens.

Say:

Many stories and fairytales have queens in them. Can you think of any? (suggest, for example, the story of Snow White) How would you act if you were **the queen in "Snow White"**? Who can show how she would **walk proudly** around the palace, showing off her beautiful hair and gown? Then show how she would **stand in front of the magic mirror** and ask who is the most beautiful of all. When the mirror answers that it is Snow White, the queen is very **angry**. How can you show that? (stamping, kicking, waving the arms)

Simlarly, the queen in "Sleeping Beauty" can be acted out: first rocking her new baby; then greeting her guests and accepting gifts from the fairies; then, when the wicked fairy appears, trying to protect the little princess; and finally falling into a deep sleep. If you want to have the children interpret entire stories, deal with one scene at a time; assign roles to the children and let them act the story as you guide them with your voice.

THE TAIL OF THE *Q*   (1–2 minutes) *locomotor*

End by having the children run around the room in one large circle, "falling flat" at your signal to make the tail of letter *Q* (see page 59).

---

18 The Letter *R*
(25–30 minutes)

Objective: To provide a letter review and vocabulary development

R IS FOR *RUN* AND *REST*   (3–3½ minutes) *locomotor*

Let the children run around freely, lying down to rest at your signals.

Say:

R is for *running* and *resting*. **Run around** wherever you like, and when I signal, (demonstrate) **lie down** in a comfortable position to **rest**. You could make believe you are sunning yourself on the beach, or taking a nap all curled up and cozy. Are you ready? Run. And rest. And run. (and so on)

Repeat 5 to 7 times.

69.

LAZY ANIMALS REACHING   (5–6 minutes) *stationary*

Start by briefly having the children reach and stretch in various ways. Then ask them to be lazy animals reaching for peanuts (see figure 69).

Say:

R is for *reaching*. How high can you reach with your **arms**? How far forward can you reach with your **nose**? How far back can you reach with one **leg**? Now **kneel** and try **reaching around yourself** in different ways and see how far you can go.

Have the children lie down and try reaching up and across with their legs. Then have them try being different animals.

Say:

Make believe you are an animal in the zoo and it is a very hot day. You feel too lazy to move, but you still want to get the peanuts people are throwing you. So you stretch yourself to reach for them. First be a **monkey** sitting and reaching with his toes and hands. Here is a peanut for you, and here's another one. Now stand up and be an **elephant**, too lazy to budge, but stretching all around with your long trunk. How many

89
The Move-Along
Alphabet

peanuts can you reach? Now be a slow-moving **sloth**, hanging upside down on a tree branch. Your legs are wrapped around the branch and you reach as far as you can with your arms.

R IS FOR *ROWING* (3–3½ minutes) *locomotor*

Have the children sit on the floor and pretend to row a boat.

Say:

 R is for *rowing*. **Make believe you are rowing a boat** across a large lake, pulling hard on the oars. (demonstrate) A gust of wind makes your boat rock back and forth. You try to keep your balance, but suddenly your **boat turns over** and **you fall in**, with a splash. Then you **climb on top** of your boat and ride over the waves back to the shore.

R IS FOR *ROBOT* (4–6 minutes) *locomotor*

Have the children pretend to be robots, moving stiffly in their own ways.

Say:

 R is for *robot*. **Make believe you are a robot.** You are very **stiff** and move very jerkily, but you can **move every part of your body in your funny, choppy way**. You can do all kinds of jobs: you can lift things and carry them; you can pull, push, dig, and sort things out. You are very strong, but sometimes you squeak and creak as you move.

After a while, have the children work in pairs to make up short skits about robots. Perhaps one child can be the operator, switching the robot on and off, and so on.

R IS FOR *LITTLE RED RIDING HOOD* (6–8 minutes) *locomotor and stationary*

Do this study in three parts:

1. The children cross the room as Little Red Riding Hood, either in a group or one at a time, picking flowers or berries. Then, on your loud signal, they see the wolf and run off.
2. The children cross the room pretending to be the wolf.
3. The children go around in a circle in twos, pretending to be Little Red Riding Hood and the wolf.

Say:

 R is for *Little Red Riding Hood*. **Come to this end of the room (indicate) and **make believe you are Little Red Riding Hood crossing the forest**, picking flowers or berries for your granny. Then when you hear my signal, (demonstrate) make believe you see the wolf and run back.

Next, have them cross as the wolf, walking with long careful steps and then making big leaps.

Say:

 Now **make believe you are the wolf**, carefully walking in and out of the trees, **sneaking quietly about**, and smiling to yourself as you think of eating up Little Red Riding Hood. Now **make big leaps** all the way across.

You may want to have them repeat both characterizations 3 or 4 times.

Ask the children to choose partners and sit down in a circle. One child is to be the wolf, the other Little Red Riding Hood. One couple at a time, the partners should go in opposite directions around the circle. When they meet, they should freeze for a moment, turn around, and go back to their places.

Say:

> **Take a partner and sit down in a circle** next to your partner. Decide who will be the wolf, and who will be Little Red Riding Hood. **One couple,** (select one) get up and turn back to back. Now **go around the circle in opposite directions,** acting out your character. Little Red Riding Hood, you can be skipping or picking flowers; wolf, you can be sneaking around with long quiet steps and a mean look on your face. **When you both meet,** stop for a moment and **freeze.** Then **turn around and run or leap back to your place,** and sit down while the next couple goes.

R IS FOR *ROCKET* AND FOR *RACE*   (2 – 2½ minutes) *locomotor*

Have the children line up against a wall (or make a line) at one end of the room and, on your signal, race to the opposite side. Start them with a countdown.

Say:

> *R* is for *rocket* and for *race.* Come to this end of the room, (indicate) and when I say go, **make believe you are a rocket racing to the moon.** (indicate where they are to run) I will count down to take-off time and then we will see who lands on the moon first. Are you ready? 5, 4, 3, 2, 1, go!

---

19 The Letter *S*
(25 – 30 minutes)

Objective: To provide a letter review and vocabulary development
Special Equipment: Polka music for sliding; soft ballet music

SLIDING SIDEWAYS   (3 – 4 minutes) *locomotor*

70.

Have the children line up on one side of the room and slide across to music. (Compare page 14.)

Say:

> **Line up** on this end of the room. When the music starts, **slide sideways** across to the other side of the room and wait there (see figure 70).

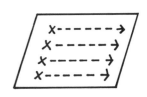

Give them a starting signal every time, letting them cross 6 to 8 times.

S IS FOR *SUN, SEA,* AND *STAR*   (4 – 5 minutes) *stationary*

Have the children spread out and then draw pictures of the sun, the sea, and the stars, changing their positions for each of these words.

Say:

> Spread out and stand comfortably. *S* is for *sun.* **Draw a large sun** in front of you, letting its rays go far out in every direction. Now sit down. *S* is also for *sea.* Make believe you are sitting on a raft in the sea, and **draw the waves around you.** Make them go high, low, and across you. Lean over

and reach to make them go out further. Now lie down. *S* is for *stars.* Make believe you are looking up into the sky at night, and **draw all the stars that you see**.

End this activity by having the children "write" the three words around themselves.

S IS FOR *SKIPPING*   (6–8 minutes) *locomotor*

Have the children take partners and make up skipping dances. If necessary, suggest a few ideas.

Say:

> *S* is for *skipping.* **Take a partner and make up a little skipping dance together.** You could hold hands and skip around each other; or you could skip one at a time, perhaps going around your partner; or you could go forward and back, and so on. Work it out, and then we will watch each couple.

S IS FOR *SARDINES*   (3–4 minutes) *stationary*

Have the children lie on the floor stretched out and very close together. Have the first in line roll off and rejoin the line at the other end, then have the next in line do the same, and so on.

Say:

> *S* is for *sardines.* **Lie down** very close together and **make believe you are sardines** in a can, packed tightly together. Now I tilt the can, and one of you **rolls off.** (indicate) You run around and join the line at the end. Now the next sardine rolls off.

Another enjoyable way of rolling like sardines is for the children to line up as before, stretched out on the floor and very close together, with both arms extended overhead. Then one child lies down at the beginning of the line, cross-wise, on top of everyone. The child just lies there passively. Then the whole row of children starts to roll in unison. This makes the child on top bump along across the whole row to the other end (see figure 71).

S IS FOR *SLEEPING BEAUTY*   (7–8 minutes) *locomotor*

Have the children work in pairs to act out the rescue of Sleeping Beauty. If possible, play background music from Tchaikovsky's ballet.

Say:

> *S* is for *Sleeping Beauty.* **Take a partner.** One of you will be Sleeping Beauty, who came under the spell of a bad fairy and fell into a deep sleep. **The other will be the gallant prince**, who **gallops** to the rescue on a big white horse. Prince, you must **fight** your way through the magic forest first. Then you find and wake your friend. Then **you both dance happily** together.

Repeat this a few times, having the partners switch roles. Then have them make a circle and take turns, one couple at a time acting out the rescue. The prince should gallop around outside the circle, and perhaps weave in and out of the seated children. Then the prince comes into the circle where Sleeping Beauty is asleep, and they dance for a short while together inside the circle.

Objective: To provide letter review and vocabulary development
Special Equipment: (both optional) Marching music or any music with a strong 4/4 beat; ballet music

T IS FOR *TRAIN* (2½–3½ minutes) *locomotor*

Have the children make a train by lining up, one behind the other, and holding on to one another's shoulders or hips.

Say:

> *T* is for *train:* **Line up**, one behind the other, and **make a long train**. The first in line will be the engine. Lead the train along on its **winding** way. When you go uphill you have to slow down and **puff along**. You can also **make stops** along the way to pick up passengers.

Repeat this 3 to 4 times, changing "engines" each time.

72.

T IS FOR *TUNNEL* (5–6 minutes) *locomotor and stationary*

Divide the class into groups of 3 or 4 children, and let each group make a tunnel.

Say:

> Take a partner and **team up with another couple**; then **make a tunnel together**, using any part of the body you like.

After each group tries out a number of things, have one group at a time make a tunnel of its choice, and have the rest of the class go through it. If necessary, suggest ideas (see figure 72).

PAINT A TEPEE (3–3½ minutes) *stationary*

Have the children stand up and write the letter *T* with bold strokes around themselves. (Compare page 56.)

Say:

> *T* is for *tepee*. **Make believe you have your own tepee** and want to decorate it with bright colors, so you **paint big letter *T*s** all over it. Make the strokes really strong so they can be seen. Splash the colors on with full force.

If you wish, you can play music as accompaniment; use any strong 4/4 beat.

T IS FOR *TABLE* (5–6 minutes) *stationary*

Have the children make different tables with their bodies (see figure 73 on page 94).

Say:

> *T* is for *table*. How could you **be a table**? How else can you make one? Try making a **high table**, then a **low one**. Then you could be a **3-legged table**, or a table standing on 1 leg.

After letting the children try out variations, suggest that they be folding tables.

Say:

> **Now be a folding table.** First you stand flat against a wall. Then I carry you into the room and lay you flat on your back. Then I pull out one leg after the other—all 4 of them. Then I turn you over and put a nice tablecloth over you and a vase of flowers.

TOUCH 2 WALLS   (2–3 minutes) *locomotor*

Have the children make a circle, note their positions, then quickly touch any 2 walls and come back to their places.

Say:

> *T* is for *touch* and for *two*. (hold up 2 fingers) We're going to play a game called Touch 2 Walls. Come and **stand in a circle**. Look to see who is standing next to you, on each side, and remember your place. When I say go, **run quickly to touch 2 walls**, at any place you like, and **hurry back** to your places. Are you ready? Go!

T IS FOR *TOYS*   (6–7 minutes) *locomotor and stationary*

Have the children pretend to be toys in a toy store, coming to life. If possible, play ballet music as background—for example, music from *Coppelia* by Delibes.

Say:

> *T* is for *toys*. **Make believe we are in a toy store and you are the toys.** At midnight **a fairy** appears and **puts life into you**. Think first what toy you would like to be. You might be Superman, or a toy train, or an electronic game, or a teddy bear, or a doll. First freeze in your positions. Now slowly wake up and move about.

End by having them all resume their original positions and then freeze.

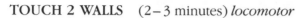

The Letter *U*
(30–35 minutes) **21**

Objective: To provide letter review and vocabulary development

U IS FOR *UPSIDE DOWN*   (6–7 minutes) *locomotor and stationary*

Have the children try out various upside-down positions in place; then have them run around, stopping to make upside-down positions at your signals (see figure 74).

Say:

> *U* is for *upside down*. **Can you look at me upside down?** (children can bend over at the waist and look through their legs, or lie down on their backs and roll their legs back toward their heads) Can you wave to me while you are upside down? What else can you do while you are upside down?

Possible actions: pointing up something; kicking a leg (either while bending forward or while lying on the back); wiggling the toes. After the children have tried these actions, continue.

Say:

 Now **run around** anywhere you like, and on my signal, (demonstrate) stop, and **turn upside down**. Try to think of a new way to turn upside down each time. Are you ready? Run. (stop) Turn upside down! And run. (and so on)

Repeat 5 or 6 times. Then continue this activity with movements in upside-down postures.

Say:

 Make a circle and **show me some of the ways you thought of to turn upside down** (see figure 75). Now, who can **bicycle** upside down? (while lying on the back) Can you **crawl** upside down? (while lying on the back) Now **walk upside down on your hands**. (bending forward)

75.

WRITE A *U* AND SHAPE A *U*   (4–5 minutes) *stationary*

Ask the children to stand in a circle. First have them draw the letter *U* around themselves. Then have them shape it with their bodies (see figure 76).

Say:

 Make believe you are standing near **a swing** that is **shaped like a U. Draw it several times** to make its outline really clear. It is a long swing, so you have to reach high up. Use both hands. Now **swing your body** up and down and from side to side, drawing the letter *U*. How would you shape a *U* with your body?

76.

Have the children try several *U*-shapes: using just the arms; using the arms and legs while lying on the back or side; lying on the stomach and curling the legs and head up; and so on. Then go on to the next activity.

77.

U IS FOR *UP*   (3–4 minutes) *locomotor*

Have the children line up on one side of the room and, one at a time, run and jump into the air.

Say:

 Everyone, line up here. (indicate) *U* is for *up*. **One at a time, run and jump up into the air.** Jump up as high as you can, but land low after your jump. Are you ready? Run. And jump up! (and so on)

U IS FOR *UNDER*   (7–8 minutes) *locomotor and stationary*

Have the children make roofs with different parts of their bodies, first individually, (see figure 77) then with partners.

Say:

U is for *under*. **Make a roof** with any part of your body. For example, you could be a house, protecting the people under your roof; or you might be a doorway with a little roof that someone could stand under when it rains; or perhaps you are a tree, making a roof with its branches and protecting the animals underneath. Try making one roof at a time and **hold your pose so we can all see it**. Then try another one.

After a while, have the children work in pairs to alternate making a roof and going under it.

Say:

Take a partner. Decide who is number 1 and who is number 2. Now all ones make a roof, and hold it so that your partner can go under it. Now change, and twos make a roof for ones to go under.

End by having all ones make roofs of their choice and all twos go under each of these all over the room; then reverse roles.

U IS FOR *UNIFORM*   (8–9 minutes) *locomotor and stationary*

First have the children name different types of people who wear uniforms. Then have them act out each one as you call out one character at a time and suggest activities for them.

Say:

U is for *uniform.* **What people** do you know of who **wear uniforms**? Now make believe you are wearing the uniform of a **police officer:** you direct traffic, blow your whistle, and walk up and down to guard the street.

Other characters and activities: a *firefighter* carrying heavy hoses, rescuing people, fighting the flames, driving the engine; a *mailcarrier* lugging a heavy sack, ringing doorbells, delivering mail, delivering birthday presents; a *nurse* fluffing someone's pillow, taking someone's temperature, giving a spoonful of medicine; a *captain of a ship* in a white uniform, looking out to sea, steering the ship, ordering the deck hands to pull the ropes to tie up the ship; a *waiter or waitress* serving food and clearing tables; a *chef;* an *airplane pilot;* a *bus driver;* and so on.

End by having the children sit in a circle and, one at a time, choose a character and act it out. They should include the other children in their portrayal.

Say:

Make a circle and sit down. One at a time, **choose one person who wears a uniform to act out.** You can **let the rest of the class help you** if you like; for example, a **mail carrier** could deliver letters to different people, or a **nurse** could take the temperatures of different patients, and so on. Who would like to start? First tell us who you are; then show us.

The Letter *V* 22
(25–30 minutes)

Objective: To provide a letter review and vocabulary development
Special Equipment: Music for skipping

V IS FOR *VICTORY*   (5–6 minutes) *locomotor*

Divide the class in half. Place the groups on opposite sides of the room, one group being dragons, the other being the heroes who fight them and then return victorious.

Say:

The letter *V* is for *victory.* **Make believe you are heroes** in a fairytale going out to **fight dragons** who are invading your land. First you fight really hard and you win. Then you return home, marching back with pride and joy, happy about your victory. The group on this side of the room (indicate) will be the heroes and heroines. The group on this side of the room (indicate) will be the dragons.

Remember that this is a make-believe battle. You don't really come close enough to touch each other. You heroines and heroes might have long magic spears or swords, which you can throw or strike with, and shields to protect yourselves. You dragons on the other side can hiss, puff, raise yourselves up and curl back down, and then blow yourselves up again, spitting fire.

Let them fight on their own for a few minutes, both groups in their own areas; then announce that the dragons have been killed and the heroes and heroines can march home victoriously.

Say:

Now **the dragons are dead**! Dragons, **puff your life out** and die. **Heroes and heroines, march around** the room, proud of your victory. Wave to the happy crowds of people; hold your swords high.

Repeat, reversing roles.

SHAPE A *V*   (5–6 minutes) *stationary*

Have the children make a circle. Ask them to shape the letter *V* with their bodies (see figure 78).

Say:

Can you **shape a *V* with your body**? Let's see how many different ideas we can find.

Let the children experiment to find as many ideas as possible; then, since there are a great many possibilities, let each child demonstrate a different way to make a *V*. After a while, let the children work in pairs to find ways to make the letter *V* (see figure 79).

V IS FOR *VOLCANO*   (3–3½ minutes) *stationary*

For a fast change of pace, let the children pretend to be volcanoes, bubbling over. Let each one decide on an initial position; then guide them with your voice, letting them move as you speak.

Say:

V is for *volcano*. Who knows what a volcano is? (discuss) **Make believe you are a volcano.** First you are **standing quietly**, a mountain with a big hump. Now the hot lava inside you **starts to boil** and rumble and churn around—and suddenly you are **bubbling over**! Hot steam and ash spurt out of you. Stones are popping out and flying high up toward the sky, and all of you is bubbling and rumbling and pouring over, rising and falling with a loud hissing noise. Then you settle down again, and cool off and stand quietly, but now your big hump is flat.

Repeat once or twice more, suggesting that they change their starting positions each time.

V IS FOR *VISIT* (6–8 minutes) *locomotor and stationary*

With the children sitting in a circle, discuss and list various places they have visited or would like to visit. Then have them take turns acting out their ideas while the rest of the class acts out the surrounding scenes.

Say:

 V is for visit. What **different places** have you visited? Where would you like to visit?

Places to visit: the zoo; a museum; a picture gallery; a friend; an amusement park; the moon; the theater; Santa at the North Pole; Sesame Street; and so on. Make a list of the places mentioned, together with notes about possible actions in each place. Then continue, letting each child pick a place to portray.

Say:

 Now **one at a time**, we will **choose a place to visit** in make-believe. First get up and tell us where you want to go to. Then **all of us will help act out the place** so that you can visit there. For example, suppose you want to visit **a museum**. We could all be statues that you could walk around and look at. Or you might want to visit the **zoo**; then we will be different animals in their cages. Or you might visit the **moon**; then we could be the rocks and craters, or perhaps winds blowing or alien creatures drifting about. Who would like to choose the first place to visit?

V IS FOR *VIRGINIA REEL* (4–5 minutes) *locomotor*

J.

Let the children take partners and line up in two lines in the center of the room. Then show them how to "cast off" (branch out, circle around, and meet again in the back; see figure J). Start by having everyone face front and put their hands on the hips or shoulders of the child in front of them. Then the lines should move—like two trains—turning away from each other and around to the back. Once the children know the pathway, let them skip forward with their partners, cast off, and meet again in the back to skip forward once again together. Stand in front of the class to direct them as each couple casts off. When all have learned the pattern, let them do it to music.

Say:

 V is for Virginia Reel. I'll show you how to do it. **Take a partner** and **line up in the center of the room**, one couple behind the other. **Come forward together; then leave your partners** and **follow the child in front of you**, turning and going all the way **to the back of the line to find your partner again**. Let's try this slowly first. Hold on to your partner and come forward. Now let go and the first couple splits off, one going this way (indicate) and the other going the other way, back to the back of the line. Find your partner again. Now everyone follow, one couple after the other.

Repeat a few more times without holding on; then let them skip to music.

The Letter *W* 23
(30–35 minutes)

Objective: To provide letter review and vocabulary development
Special Equipment: Masking tape or chalk

W IS FOR *WALKING*   (3–4 minutes) *locomotor*

Have the children walk freely, changing pace and steps according to your directions. Use a percussive beat after each call to alert the children to the change.

Say:

 W is for *walking.* Walk around, and on my signal stop and listen for my next call. Ready? **Walk**. (stop) Walk **fast**. (stop) Walk very **slowly**. (stop) Walk **backward**. (and so on)

Other calls: walk on *tiptoes;* walk *sideways;* walk on your *heels;* walk *sideways the other way;* walk *backward* fast; take *giant steps* forward; walk on *all fours;* walk *around yourself;* walk with *stiff legs* like a toy, with *floppy legs* like Raggedy Ann or Andy; walk on *3 legs* like a lame bear; walk like a *wriggly* puppy; and so on.

W IS FOR *WINDOW* AND *WAVING*   (4–6 minutes) *locomotor and stationary*

Review briefly making windows with different parts of the body (see page 18). Then divide the class: one half will make windows, the other half will wave through them.

Say:

W is for *window.* Do you remember **making windows with different parts of your body**? Show me a few. Remember that you can lie, stand, or be in any position you wish. *W* is also for *waving.* Now this half of the group, (indicate) spread out a bit and make any window you like. You can change to different windows whenever you like. The rest of the class, wander around and wave through as many windows as you wish. You can make believe you are waving to a friend, or you may pretend to wave something out of the window—a flag, a handkerchief, a scarf, or even a balloon.

Call for a change of roles. Then end by having the children be rugs, which are shaken out of the window (see figure 80).

Say:

Make believe you are a small rug, and I am shaking you out of the window. First I lift you up and hang you over the ledge. Then I shake you up and down to get the dust out of you. Then I wiggle you and bounce you some more. Then I stretch you up high to get a good look at you. Finally I put you flat on the floor.

Repeat once or twice. The children can bob up and down, bending forward, as well as swing from side to side.

W IS FOR *WASHING MACHINE*   (3–4 minutes) *stationary*

Have the children make believe they are washing machines; guide them with your voice as they move (see figure 81).

Say:

W is for *washing machine.* **Make believe you are a washing machine** standing square and solid in the kitchen or basement. Now I turn you on, and slowly you start to work. You **swish the clothes** back and forth, rubbing and scrubbing them in different places. You **turn all around**, swishing and churning to get the clothes clean. Swish the clothes back and forth, up and down, pull and push, turn them around. You **splash the soap suds** all around, making everything full of bubbles. Now you **rinse**

continued

99
The Move-Along
Alphabet

81. *continued*

the **bubbles** away and squeeze the clothes dry. You **twist and bend**, reaching high and low, squeezing hard. Finally you **spin them around** and around. Then you stop and **rest**.

WALKING OUT A *W*   (6–7 minutes) *locomotor*

Mark out a large *W* on the floor with masking tape or chalk. Then let the children walk the figure out in ways suggested by words that start with the letter *W* (see figure K).

Say:

> **Make one long line** here. (indicate) Let's **walk over this *W*** using words that start with a *W*. One after the other, **waddle** like a duck. Now **wander** along it as if you were in the woods, looking for your way. Now **watch** your steps carefully as if you were walking on a wall.

Other *W*-words: **wading** along a winding river; **wobbling** along with stiff knees; sliding along on your knees as if you were a **walrus**; sniffing and listening as if you were a **wolf**; swimming as if you were a **whale**, spurting water at every corner; skimming along as if you were a **witch** riding a broomstick, jumping off at the end with a loud **"whee!"**

W IS FOR *WISHING WELL*   (7–8 minutes) *locomotor and stationary*

Have the children sit in a circle. Then have them take turns getting up to make a wish for some gift or toy. Each child should then move around the circle with his or her make-believe item, pretending to use or play with it. Start the children out with suggestions.

Say:

K.

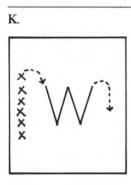

> **Make a circle and sit down.** There is a story that at the edge of a mountain there is a well called the *Wishing Well*. If you look into it during the full moon and make a wish, your wish comes true. Make believe this wishing well is right inside our circle. **One at a time, get up and make a wish** for a toy or a special thing you would like to have; then take it out of the wishing well and **move around the circle with it.** For example, you might wish for a **ball**, or a **jump rope**, or a pet to cuddle and lead around. Or perhaps **silver slippers** that make you dance, or **ice skates**, or maybe even a pretty **dress** that spreads out when you twirl. One at a time, everyone can think of something to wish for, and then go to fish it out of the wishing well.

Let the children take their turns in consecutive order. If the group is small enough, repeat the activity to give each child 2 or 3 wishes.

W IS FOR *WITCH*   (2–3 minutes) *locomotor*

End this session with everyone doing a witch's dance in unison.

Say:

> Everyone up on your feet. **Be a witch** once again, riding on your broomstick through the windy sky. Or you might be witches dancing around a fire, stirring your magic brews and laughing at the world.

End by having everyone freeze in a witchy position.

Objective: To provide letter reviews and vocabulary development

Special Equipment: A name card for each child

X IS AT THE END OF *SIX*   (4–5 minutes) *locomotor*

Have the children cross from one side of the room to the other, using steps suggested by the children, repeating each step 6 times.

Say:

> Today we have the last 3 letters of the alphabet: *X, Y,* and *Z. X* is at the end of *six.* (write the word *six* on the board) Move to this end of the room (indicate), and **one at a time suggest a step** for all of us to do. We'll **repeat it 6 times**.

Possible steps: 6 hops on one leg; 6 jumps with both feet together; 6 marching steps; 6 turns; 6 big leaps; 6 skips; 6 jumping jacks; 6 backward steps; 6 sideways steps; 6 backward jumps; 6 sideways sliding steps; 6 frog jumps; 6 gallops; and so on.

82.

Y IS FOR *YEAR*   (5–7 minutes) *locomotor and stationary*

Discuss the different seasons of the year; then take one season at a time and let the class make a number of activities appropriate to each.

Say:

> *Y* is for *year.* How many seasons are there in a year? (list them) What happens in spring? (plants sprouting, animals coming out of furrows to sun themselves, birds building nests and twittering happily, and so on) **Make believe it is spring** and you are the little seedling of a plant, sprouting new leaves. Or be a bear who was asleep all winter and who's just waking up to the sunshine.

Continue with the other seasons in a similar way.

- Summer: Vacations, playing on the beach or near a pond, rolling in the grass, Fourth of July, and so on.
- Autumn: Leaves falling and blowing about, trees swaying in the wind and rain, fruit ripening (picking berries, apples), Halloween.
- Winter: Playing in the snow, ice skating, being Santa riding on his sleigh, giving and getting gifts, and so on.

End by letting each child choose one season of the year and act out his or her favorite interpretation of it.

Z IS FOR *ZIPPER*   (3–4 minutes) *stationary*

Have the children sit in a circle. Ask them to pretend they have zippers they can use to open and close different parts of their bodies.

Say:

> *Z* is for *zipper.* **Make believe you have zippers between your fingers.** Can you zip and unzip them? Now you have a zipper **between both hands**. How would you zip it and unzip it? How could you **zip up your arms?** Find different ways. (vertically, horziontally, behind the back, and so on)

continued

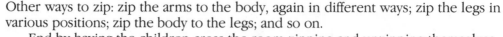

Other ways to zip: zip the arms to the body, again in different ways; zip the legs in various positions; zip the body to the legs; and so on.

End by having the children cross the room zipping and unzipping themselves.

Say:

> Everyone **come to this end of the room**, (indicate and **zip your whole self up**. When I say go, **start across the room, unzipping yourself** as you go. You should be unzipped and open when you get to the other side. Ready? Run! Now **run back again, this time zipping yourself up** as you go.

Repeat this, letting them strike a different position each time (see figure 82).

X IS AT THE END OF *MIX*   (7 – 8 minutes) *locomotor and stationary*

Write out name cards for each of the children. Have them sit in a circle, and put the cards in a sack or box in the middle. Each child in turn should pick a card at random and write out the letters of the name on it in a any way they like. The others should try to guess the name.

Say:

> Let's take the letter *X* once again. Here it is at the end of *mix*. (write the word *mix* on the chalkboard) Here are all your names — I'll mix them up. **One at a time, fish out a card and look at it secretly** so no one can read it except you. Then **write out each letter** in the name you drew, **any way you like.** You can use one part of your body to write the whole name, or you can use different parts to write different letters. You can even walk out a letter. Use your own ideas for each letter, and we will guess what name you have picked.

Choose a child to start. Have the child whose name was picked take the next turn, and so on. Ask the children not to make guesses until the whole name has been "written."

X IS FOR *X-MAS*   (7 – 8 minutes) *locomotor and stationary*

Have the children work in groups of 4 or 5 to make up scenes pertaining to X-mas.

Say:

> *X* is for *X-mas,* which is short for Christmas. Take a partner and then get together with another couple to **make up a scene about *X-mas.***

Walk around while the children are working, and suggest ideas, if necessary.

Ideas for scenes: Santa with his reindeer; writing to Santa, going to bed and finding a gift on Christmas morning; decorating a tree; unwrapping presents and playing with them (some children could be the toys); shopping for toys (some children could be toys in a shop window); and so on.

When all are ready, let them take turns to show their scenes.

From *A* to *Z* in Nature 25
(30 – 35 minutes)

Objectives: To provide movement fun through make believe; increase vocabulary development

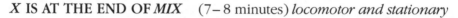

Note: This is a supplementary lesson, covering all the letters of the alphabet, with nature as its central theme. The activities range from 30 seconds to 3 minutes in length. Most of them require no specific preparation.

A IS FOR *APPLES* AND *APPLE CART*

After a brief discussion of nature's pervasiveness and importance in the world, have the children take partners and make "wheelbarrows," with one child walking on the hands and the other holding on to the "wheelbarrow's" ankles (see figure 83). If the children are small, they should take turns being the wheelbarrow and you should carry their ankles. Or you may want to substitute "A is for Apples" (page 63).

Say:

> Nature is everywhere around us. We are all part of nature. Let's go through the alphabet to find words about nature for each of the letters. *A* is for *apples*. **Make believe we are in an apple orchard**, shaking trees and picking the apples up and wheeling them away in a wheelbarrow. **Take a partner.** One of you be the cart or **wheelbarrow** full of apples, and the other one be the **farmer** who pushes you all the way home.

B IS FOR *BEES*

Have the children keep their partners. One of them should be a flower; the other should be a buzzing bee that flies to all the other flowers in the room. After a minute or so, have the bees and flowers reverse roles.

Say:

> Stay with your **partners**, and one of you be a **flower** while the other is a **bee** buzzing around. All bees, go all over the room to any flower you like to collect your honey. Now come back to your partners and change roles.

Continue with the next series of activities in fairly rapid succession.

Say:

> *C* is for *crocodile.* Everyone stretch out on the floor and be a crocodile, opening and closing your long green jaws. Your arms can be your jaws.
> *D* is for *donkey.* Trot around the room being a donkey, pulling your cart over a winding mountain path.
> *E* is for *earth.* Make believe you are a mole digging a hole for yourself in the soft earth, making a little molehill. When you are done, look out of the doorway of your cozy earth house.
> *F* is for *frog.* Who can jump like a frog?
> *G* is for *grass.* Make believe you are jumping and playing on nice soft grass. When you get tired, stretch out and enjoy the fresh smell and the sound of the wind rustling through the blades.
> *H* is for *hill.* Make believe you are climbing up a steep hill, and when you reach the top you roll back down.
> *I* is for *icicle.* Be a frozen icicle standing long and stiff and glittering in the sunshine. Now, bit by bit, you melt.
> *J* is for *jellyfish.* Make believe you are a soft, round jellyfish floating about and groping round with your long soft arms.
> *K* is for *kangaroo.* Hop like a kangaroo with its baby in its pouch.
> *L* is for *lizard.* Can you be a lizard crawling on the rocks? Sun yourself on the warm stones as you turn your head around to look around you.
> *M* is for *mist,* covering the mountain. Make believe you are mist in the

early morning, slowly rising from the ground and spreading over the countryside, rising higher and higher as you move along until you stretch your long arms to the very top of the mountain.

N is for *nature* itself. Come and sit in a circle and tell me what you like best when you think of nature.

Let the children take a short rest as they tell about the things they like in nature. Suggest a number of things, bringing the beauty of nature into the discussion whenever possible. Examples: sunlight on a silver lake; cornfields rustling in the breeze; dew drops glittering on the grass in the early morning; a rainbow; a thunderstorm, with clouds racing over the sky; the smell of a forest after a rain; the songs of birds; the stillness of a forest.

After a while, continue with the next series of activities.

Say:

Which letter comes after *N*? The letter *O*! *O* is for *ocean*. Be anything you like that has to do with the ocean.

P is for *puddles*. Make believe the room is full of puddles, and jump over as many as you can.

Q is for *quake,* as when the earth quakes. Make believe you are a volcano. Your hot lava is grumbling and bubbling and making you quake.

R is for *river*. Line up and, one after the other, run and jump over a river.

S is for *snow* and *slush*. Make believe you are wading around in deep snow and sliding in the slush.

T is for *tulip*. Be a tulip bulb slowly growing into a beautiful flower.

U is for *universe*. Climb into your spaceship and fly around the universe. Now turn around and come back home, landing with a crash.

V is for *vulture*. Now you are a big vulture circling up into the sky, looking for food with your sharp eyes. You almost never flap your wings. You just float easily on the wind until you come to a high bare cliff. You land on it and fold your wings and look out over the mountaintops.

W is for *wind*. Make believe there is a strong wind and it is blowing you around in gusts.

X is at the end of *ox*. An ox is a very big, strong, helpful animal something like a cow. Be an ox grazing in the fields or pulling a loaded cart with slow, heavy steps, bowing your head as you walk.

Y is for *yellow,* the color of lemons. Make believe you are a lemon and I'm squeezing the juice out of you.

Z is for *zebra*. Gallop around the room like a zebra in the wide open fields. Now you come to a lake. You stop to graze and have a drink, and you look at your stripes in the water.

APPENDIX
Glossary of Movement Terms

Body isolations: Moving the various parts of the body separately; moving, for example, only the fingers or only one leg.

Dynamics of movement: The combined elements of force and time. Changing or adding either of these elements to a movement results in a completely different movement experience.

Force (as an element pertaining to movement): The energy used to produce movement; it can be light, heavy, soft, strong, sharp, smooth, weak, hard, relaxed, tense, loose, or tight.

Interpretations: Studies in which children identify with an object or character, assume its qualities, and act it out, adding their own ideas to the impersonation.

Isolations: See Body isolations.

Locomotor activities: Activities that involve moving through space (walking, running, skipping, and so on).

Movement education: Teaching the control and understanding of body moves in combination with the various elements of time, space, and force.

Space (as an element pertaining to movement): The area in which movement takes place, incorporating direction, dimension, level, shape, form, pattern, pathway, and focus of motion.

Stationary activities: Activities done in place, either from a standing position, or while sitting or lying on the floor.

Time (as an element pertaining to movement): The pace and/or rhythm of a motion, variously fast, slow, long, short, even, uneven, sustained, held, pausal, or modulated.

Warm-up: An opening activity, usually a brisk locomotor one, designed to put the body in a state of readiness for more sustained physical activity.

Workout: A combination of physical activities that exercises the entire body. As such, it is a desirable goal of each lesson.

Glossary
of Musical Terms
(to help in the selection of recorded music)

Adagio: In a slow tempo; literally, at ease. The second movement of a symphony or sonata is usually adagio. In ballet suites an adagio is usually a lyrical, romantic piece with a flowing melody. Adagios are particularly useful as background music for slow-paced interpretations.

Allegro: In a fairly fast tempo; lively.

Andante: In a medium tempo; literally, walking.

Coda: The ending part of a composition. Often, and especially in ballets, the coda is in a very fast tempo. Thus it can be useful as accompaniment to fast runs, gallops, and so on.

Divertimento or divertissement: A series of separate, unconnected short pieces; for example, in "Aurora's Wedding" (Act III of *Sleeping Beauty* by Tchaikovsky).

Minuet: A graceful old French dance in 3/4 time; daintier than a waltz. It is sometimes used in the third movement of a symphony or sonata.

Moderato: In a moderate tempo.

Movement: The separate parts of a musical composition. There may be three or four movements in a symphony, sonata, concerto, and so on, each listed according to its tempo and mood.

Pizzicato: Part of a composition using short separate notes, usually played by plucking strings, rather than playing them with a bow. A pizzicato is useful as accompaniment to walking daintily on tiptoes, running lightly, and making small light jumps (as in interpretations of elves, fairies, birds).

Polka: A lively folk dance, originally Bohemian, in 2/2 or 2/4 time; useful for brisk locomotor activities such as skipping or running freely.

Presto: At a fast tempo.

Scherzo: A humorous, lively composition, usually in fairly fast 3/4 time, with strong accents. It is sometimes used in the third movement of a symphony or sonata. A scherzo is good for lively character interpretations such as clowns, washing machines, popcorn, and so on.

Waltz: A smooth dance in moderate 3/4 time; very good as accompaniment for flowing, drawn-out movements and interpretations such as flowers, butterflies, clouds, and so on.

Recommended Recordings for Movement Accompaniment

Activity and Funtime Songs (Golden): Short, cute, vocalized songs in good rhythms. Good for circle games or as general locomotor accompaniment.

American Jigs and Reels (Folkways): Good for skipping, running, and other fast locomotor activities. Use this or any available recording of jigs and reels.

Ballet Music: Use excerpts from any available recordings. Especially recommended is music by Tchaikovsky (*The Nutcracker Suite, The Sleeping Beauty*) and Delibes (*Coppelia, Sylvia*). These provide "variations" (short dances) in different tempos and moods.

    The slower parts (adagios, panoramas, and other descriptive scenes) are particularly good as background for slower-paced interpretations.

Dances from Old Vienna: Use any available recordings. These dances include music by Mozart, Haydn, Schubert, Strauss, Beethoven, and others, with compositions ranging from waltzes to gallops, landlers, minuets, and so on.

    Provides worthwhile musical accompaniment for moderately paced activities. (See also Waltzes and Folk Dances)

Electronic Music: See *The In Sound from Way Out* and *The Amazing New Electronic Pop Sound*.

Folk Dance Party for Everyone (Evelyn Halper, Cotillion): A selection of simple rhythmic dances from various countries. Good for general warm-up activities such as skipping, walking, and so on.

Folk Dances: Use any available recordings. Recommended are round dances from England, jigs and reels from Ireland and Scotland, and albums of dances from Vienna and Switzerland. These provide a wide variety of lively dances such as waltzes, gallops, marches, landlers, polkas, and schottisches. Excellent for all brisk locomotion.

Folk Tunes & Music of the Masters. (Adapted for the classroom, Elise Braun-Barnett American Montessori Society): Very nice selection of short rhythmic piano excerpts, designed for brisk movement activities for small children. Excellent and useful for a variety of activities, including circle activities such as follow the leader, and one-at-a-time moving around the circle.

Make Believe in Movement (Maya Doray, Kimbo Educational): Seven selected interpretations with music and narration. Side 2: music only. Manual included.

Designed as accompaniment for movement activities with small children.

Move Along Alphabet (Maya Doray, Kimbo Educational): Short, imaginative interpretations and movement studies, one for each letter of the alphabet. Narration with music. Manual included.

Designed as accompaniment for movement activities with small children.

Music for Children to Dance to (Mitch Miller, Golden): Melodic, fairly short pieces with even rhythms, adapted from classical and folk repertoire. Nice background for various interpretations or movement studies.

Polkas: Use any available recordings, preferably nonvocal. Especially nice are those from Vienna, Sweden, and Switzerland. See also Folk Dances. Good for skipping, sliding, and other brisk activities.

Sound Effects: Use any available recordings. Look for short bands with a great variety of noises. Good for special effects for interpretations such as ghosts, wind, rain, and so on.

The Amazing New Electronic Pop Sound of J. J. Perrey (Vanguard): Very cute rhythmic pieces in various tempos. Excellent for interpretations such as machines, popcorn, mechanical toys, and so on.

The In Sound from Way Out: Electronic Pop Music (Perrey-Kingsley, Vanguard): Similar to the preceding listing, and by the same author. Equally excellent.

Waltzes: Use any available recordings. Especially recommended are those by the Strauss family of Vienna (Johann Sr. and Jr., Josef, and Eduard); those on Swiss folk dance recordings, and those from ballets. Suitable for all gentle, moderately paced interpretations and movement studies with a flowing quality, such as butterflies, clouds, and other scenes from nature, and so on.

Selecting
Recordings

Whenever possible, use classicial music to accompany movement sessions. The music of Mozart, Schubert, Schumann, Haydn, Beethoven, Tchaikovsky, and many others is excellent to move to, and is always enjoyed by children. Moveover, such music is melodious and tends to provide an even tempo without an overpowering beat.

When buying records for movement accompaniment, specifically records of classical and ballet music, make sure that there are separate bands for all the various parts. For example the ballet music from the *Nutcracker Suite* by Tchaikovsky consists of an overture, a march, the "Dance of the Sugar Plum Fairy," and several more dances in various tempos and moods. On some recordings the pauses between dances are too brief to be visible, making it very difficult or impossible to pick out the part you want to use. Similarly, symphonies and sonatas have separate parts or movements, and on some records the movements are clearly separated by pauses. If you cannot find such a recording, you are better off with excerpts, which are sure to have separate bands for each segment.

You should be guided in your choice of music mainly by your own ear and your own taste. The following lists of records are offered as guidelines to help you find particular kinds of music for particular purposes.

Suggestions
for Related Reading

Creative Movement for the Developing Child. Clare Cherry. Belmont, CA: Pitman Learning, 1971.

Creative Rhythmic Movement for Children. Gladys Andrews. Englewood Cliffs, NJ: Prentice Hall, Inc., 1954.

Dance in Elementary Education. Ruth L. Murray. New York: Harper & Row, 1970.

First Steps in Teaching Creative Dance. Mary Joyce. Palo Alto, CA: National Press Books, 1973.

Meditation with Children — the Art of Concentration and Centering. Deborah Rozman. Boulder Creek, CA: University of the Trees Press, 1975.

INDEX

Doorways, 16
Dragons, 96–98
Dream, 68
Drop down, 8, 68

E
E, 69–70
Earth, 103
Egg, 69
Elevator, 70
Engine, 69
Exercise, 69

F
F, 70–72
Factory, 71
Fairy, 31
Family, 71
Floating, 32, 70
Follow the leader, 4
Forward and backward, 5–7
Freeze, run and, 9; move and, 33
Friend, meeting a, 4
Frog, 71, 103
Funny, 72

G
G, 58, 72–73
Gallop, 58, 72
Game, 73
Garden, 73
Ghost, 73
Giant, 30–32, 73
Grass, 103
Growing, 72

H
H, 73–74
Half-circle, 44–46
Halloween, 74
Heavy and light, 30–32, 53
Hello, saying, 4
Heroes, 96–98
Hill, 103
Hopping, 2
Horse, 73
House, 74
Hurry, 74

I
I, 39–42, 75–76
Icicle, 103

Initial, 59
Ink, 41–42
Inside, 75
Inviting, 76
Island, 75

J
J, 49–51, 76–78
Jack and Jill, 77
Jack-in-the-box, 17, 77
Jellyfish, 51, 103
Jerking, 76
Jogging, 76
Juice, 77
Jump, 77
Jumping jacks, 15

K
K, 78–79
Kaleidoscope, 79
Kangaroo, 78, 103
Kicking, 78
Kitchen, 78
Kittens, 5

L
L, 79–81
Leader, follow the, 4, 80
Legs, 80
Letter sounds, 32–34
Lightly, 79
Line, 80
Lizard, 103
Long and short, 27–30
Love, 80

M
M, 81–82
Machines, 25
Magic, 81
Marionettes, 12
Meeting a friend, 4, 82
Merry-go-round, 82
Mirror, 81
Mist, 103
Mole, 103
Move and freeze game, 33, 43
Moving, 81

N
N, 82–84
Name games, 25–27

ABOUT
THE AUTHOR

A nationally known specialist in movement education, Maya B. Doray is the author of *See What I Can Do!*, a book of creative movement for children (Prentice-Hall). She has performed with dance companies in the United States, London, Rome, and New York and has taught creative movement and dance to children and adults. For the past few years, she has toured the United States giving workshops at colleges of education. She has made two records: *Make Believe In Movement* and *Move Along Alphabet* (Kimbo Education) and has choreographed, directed, and produced many children's shows.